Christmas
Cats and Dogs

Christmas Cats and Dogs

Quilts to Celebrate the Season

~~~~~ Janet Kime ~~~~~

Martingale™
& COMPANY

Credits

President • Nancy J. Martin
CEO • Daniel J. Martin
Publisher • Jane Hamada
Editorial Director • Mary V. Green
Managing Editor • Tina Cook
Technical Editor • Barbara Weiland
Copy Editor • Liz McGehee
Art Director • Stan Green
Illustrator • Laurel Strand
Cover and Text Designer • Regina Girard
Photographer • Brent Kane

That Patchwork Place® is an imprint of
Martingale & Company™.

Christmas Cats and Dogs: Quilts to Celebrate the Season
© 2002 by Janet Kime

Martingale & Company
20205 144th Avenue NE
Woodinville, WA 98072-8478 USA
www.martingale-pub.com

Printed in Hong Kong
07 06 05 04 03 02   8 7 6 5 4 3 2 1

Mission Statement

We are dedicated to providing quality products and service by working together to inspire creativity and to enrich the lives we touch.

Library of Congress Cataloging-in-Publication Data

Kime, Janet
    Christmas cats and dogs: quilts to celebrate the season / Janet Kime.
        p. cm.
    ISBN 1-56477-422-8
    1. Patchwork—Patterns. 2. Quilted goods.
3. Christmas decorations. 4. Cats in art. 5. Dogs in art.
I. Title
TT835 .K55 2002
746.46' 041—dc21   2002003478

Contents

Introduction

Collected in the pages of this book are holiday designs featuring cats and dogs—humankind's favorite companions. The quilted projects range in size from large quilts to small wall hangings. Some are speed-pieced (no templates required!), some are appliquéd, and some are made with a combination of both techniques. A redwork project is also included for those of you who love embroidery.

In addition, you'll find directions for Christmas stockings in a range of sizes, a beribboned garland of kittens in holiday dresses, and a wreath of yo-yo cats. As a special Christmas gift to my readers, I've also included instructions for converting many of the designs into ornaments to hang on your tree or around the house, or to use as package decorations.

Just to prove that holiday quilts don't have to be red and green, you'll find several other festive color combinations. No matter which project you choose, feel free to adapt the colors to suit your own decor—soft green and rose, deep blues and silver, hot pink and lime green, pastel country plaids—these are only a few of the possibilities.

I hope this book inspires you to create quilts and decorations that will bring a smile to your face as you prepare for the holidays and honor your favorite feline or trusty dog.

General Directions

The following basic quiltmaking directions are included for your reference when making any of the quilts or projects in this book. Refer to them as needed to create a quilt with professional results.

Choosing Fabrics

In general, I try to use only 100 percent cottons in my quilted projects. Blends are more difficult to handle—they're slippery, they are often more loosely woven than traditional quilting cottons and stretch out of shape, and it is difficult to get a sharp crease when you press them. It's especially important to use only 100 percent–cotton fabrics for quilts that will be washed repeatedly; cottons will fade faster than blends, and as the quilt "mellows," the blends will tend to look harsh against the softening cotton tones.

It's OK to include other kinds of fabrics in small wall hangings and Christmas decorations that won't be laundered. If you like glitter and shine in your holiday projects, experiment with silks, satins, velvets, and some of the wonderful metallic fabrics that are available. If you've been doing all of your fabric shopping in quilt shops, stop by a fashion fabric store and wander through the evening and bridal fabrics for inspiration. Just be aware that these specialty fabrics can be more difficult to tame than 100 percent cottons. Be careful when you press them. Some fibers melt at the temperatures used to press cottons.

Machine Piecing

Maintaining an accurate ¼"-wide seam allowance is extremely important when machine piecing. If seams aren't accurate, the seam lines of the designs won't match up, the points of your triangles won't be pointed, the blocks won't fit together properly, and the whole piece won't lie flat.

On many sewing machines, the edge of the presser foot is exactly ¼" from the needle. On some machines, the needle position is adjustable. On other machines, you'll need to make a ¼" seam guide by placing masking tape on the throat plate.

Check your machine with a piece of ¼" graph paper. Cut the paper along one of the grid lines. Slip the paper under the presser foot and lower the needle onto the line ¼" from the cut edge. If the cut edge isn't exactly at the edge of the presser foot, place a piece of masking tape along the cut edge of the paper to mark your ¼" seam guide.

Test the accuracy of your ¼" seams by sewing a pieced block and measuring it. Even if you appear to be making accurate ¼" seams, your block may be too small. This happens because a little of the fabric is taken up by the bump that forms where each seam allowance is pressed. Most quilters find they need to take a seam allowance that is just a thread or two under ¼"—a *scant* ¼" seam.

Pressing

Careful and thorough pressing is one of the most important aspects of quiltmaking. There are two basic pressing rules to follow when you machine stitch quilt blocks.

1. Press all seam allowances to one side.
2. Always press each seam *before* crossing it with another seam. Pressing seam allowances to one side takes less time than pressing them open, and this method of pressing also makes for a stronger quilt top. (Think about how much easier it is to rip out a seam that's been pressed open than one that's pressed to one side.)

Press on the wrong side of the piece to set the stitches into the fabric, and then press the seam to one side. On the right side, push the broad side of the iron against the "bump" of the seam line to flatten it as much as possible.

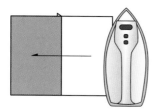

Pressing the seam allowances to one side also allows you to press matching seams in opposite directions. This makes it easier to butt the seam lines against each other for more accurate matching at seam intersections.

The illustrations in this book include arrows that indicate the correct pressing direction for each seam to ensure easy, accurate piecing. When it isn't necessary to match seams, the pressing arrows indicate the direction that will best reduce bulk. Occasionally, seams are pressed open to reduce bulk.

Rotary Cutting

You will need at least three pieces of equipment to cut the pieces for the quilts in this book: a rotary cutter, a cutting mat designed for rotary cutters, and one or two transparent acrylic rulers. (You will also need sharp scissors for cutting the appliqués.) Follow these simple steps to ensure accurately cut pieces for your project.

1. Press your fabric before cutting to remove all wrinkles. Fold it with selvages together and lay it on the cutting mat with the fold toward you.
2. If you don't have a second ruler, place the folded fabric edge on one of the grid lines on the mat. Then line up your long ruler with a vertical grid line so that the ruler just covers the raw edges of the fabric. If you have a second ruler, place it close to the left edge of the fabric and align the edge of the ruler with the fold. Lay the long ruler next to the short ruler so that it just covers the raw edges of the fabric, and then remove the short ruler.
3. Cut the fabric with the rotary cutter, rolling the blade away from you along the side of the long ruler. This first cut is called a clean-up cut. It tidies the edge of your fabric and ensures that the next cut will be exactly perpendicular to the fold. If the cuts aren't perpendicular to the fold, the strips won't be perfectly straight when you open them. Instead, they will have a dogleg jog, and the next cuts won't be accurate either. It's a good idea to check the angle of the ruler after every two or three cuts and to make another clean-up cut whenever necessary.

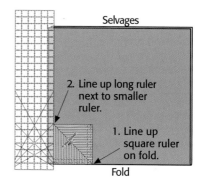

4. After you've tidied up the edge of the fabric, you're ready to cut the pieces for your quilt. Align the required measurement on the ruler with the newly cut edge of the fabric. Cut strips across the width of the fabric, from selvage to selvage, in the required width, unless directed otherwise in individual quilt directions.

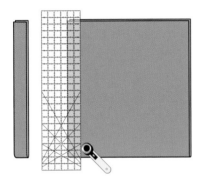

5. Trim away the selvage ends and crosscut the strips into pieces of the desired size. For example, if the directions call for 4 squares, 4" x 4", cut a 4"-wide strip across the width of the fabric, trim off the selvages, and make 2 crosscuts, 4" wide.

Speed Piecing

Speed piecing is a combination of rotary cutting and shortcut sewing techniques that make your preparation and actual sewing a lot faster and easier.

Making Strip Units

Many speed-pieced designs require a strip unit, which is made by sewing fabric strips together lengthwise. The strip unit is pressed and then cross-cut into segments. The segments are sewn together to make the block or a portion of the block.

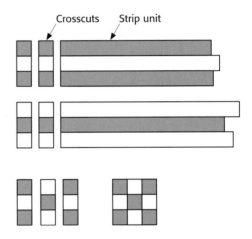

Flip-and-Sew Piecing

Use this speed-piecing method to assemble quilt-block sections that would otherwise require templates.

1. Lay one piece on top of the other at right angles, right sides together, and draw a diagonal line with a ruler as shown. Sew on the drawn line.

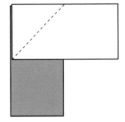

2. Trim away the excess fabric, leaving about ¼" for a seam allowance. Press the seam allowance in the direction indicated by the arrows in the illustrations for the quilt you are making (usually, but not always, toward the darker color).

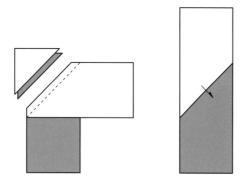

Note: Whenever there is a choice, start stitching the diagonal at the edge of the bottom layer of fabric; it's easier than starting at the point.

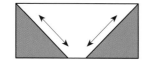

The unit may distort as you press it. If this happens, pull it back into shape by grasping the ends of the stitched diagonal line and pulling gently.

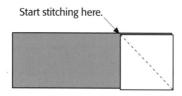

If piece is curved, pull along direction of arrows to straighten.

Making Half-Square-Triangle Units

The half-square-triangle unit is common in pieced designs. It's traditionally made by sewing two half-square triangles together to make a square. In addition, there are a number of techniques for speed piecing half-square-triangle units. Any book with instructions for rotary-cut quilts includes at least one method. My favorite follows.

1. Cut 2 squares the same size (as indicated in the specific directions for the quilt you are making). Draw a diagonal line on the wrong side of one of the squares (best done on the lighter color for better visibility).

2. Place the squares right sides together. Sew a scant ¼" from the line on both sides.

3. Cut on the diagonal line. You'll have 2 half-square-triangle units. Press the seam allowances toward the darker fabric in each unit, unless the directions indicate otherwise.

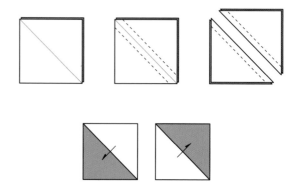

Adding Appliqués

I recommend the paper-patch method of appliqué. Although it takes a little time to prepare each piece, even beginners can achieve smooth curves and precise shapes with this method.

Note: The appliqué templates in this book *do not* include turn-under allowances; you must add them as you cut out each piece.

1. Trace the appliqué template on paper and cut out exactly on the drawn line. Trace around the template on a piece of lightweight card stock or construction paper. Cut out the paper piece carefully, making any curves as smooth as possible. Refer to the illustration of the quilt and label the *right side* of each paper piece.

Cat Chat

Tracing Appliqué Templates

If you need to cut numerous pieces from one template, trace it onto template plastic rather than paper. If you trace around a paper template many times, the edge will fray and it will be difficult to make accurate patches.

2. Place the paper piece *right side down* on the *wrong side* of the fabric and pin. Cut out the fabric shape, adding a ¼"-wide allowance all around the paper piece.

3. Fold the allowance under and baste it in place, sewing through the paper piece and making the fabric as smooth as possible around the curves.

The finished piece should be quite taut over the paper shape. Clip around inside curves almost to the paper piece. Make the clips at least ¼" apart or the fabric will fray.

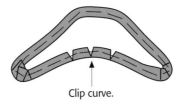

Clip curve.

When you come to a corner, baste one edge down all the way to the corner, and then fold the other edge over it and continue basting.

4. After basting the paper patch, press it thoroughly. Do not remove the basting or the paper yet.

5. Position the appliqué on the background fabric as directed for the quilt you are making and sew in place, using a thread color that matches the appliqué, *not* the background fabric. Catch just a few threads at the edge of the piece. Only a tiny stitch should show on the front of the quilt; all the "stitch traveling" is done on the wrong side.

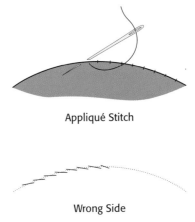

Appliqué Stitch

Wrong Side

6. Stitch almost all the way around the paper patch, leaving 1" to 2" unstitched along a straight edge. Remove the basting threads, and then reach in and pull out the paper. If the paper tears, use a pair of tweezers to pull out any fragments.

Remove paper patch.

Note: Some quilters prefer to sew all the way around the appliqué piece and then make a slit in the background fabric behind the patch to remove the paper. The slit can be left open; the stitching all around the paper patch will stabilize the area.

7. After you've removed all the paper, finish sewing the appliqué in place.

Assembling the Quilt Top

After your blocks are completed, you are ready to arrange them and sew them together to make the quilt top.

1. Sew the quilt blocks together in horizontal rows. Press the seam allowances of the first row in one direction, the seam allowances of the second row in the other direction, and so on.

Dog Talk

Transferring Appliqué Designs

The center of each appliqué design in this book is marked with a small cross to help you position the pieces correctly on your quilt squares.

1. To find and mark the center of a quilt square, fold it in half crosswise and finger-press the fold. Open the square, fold in half in the opposite direction, and finger-press again.

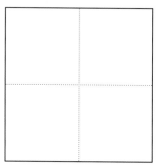

2. Place the center of the square over the cross and lightly mark the positions of each appliqué piece. If you can't see the design through your background fabric, photocopy the design and tape it to a window. Tape your background fabric over the design and lightly trace it with a pencil.

2. Sew the rows together and press the seams in the direction of least resistance.

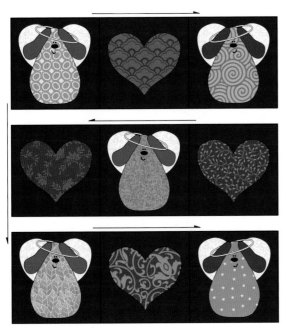

Press seams in opposite directions
from row to row.

Some quilts have sashing strips between the blocks for added interest. If so, press all seams toward the sashing strips.

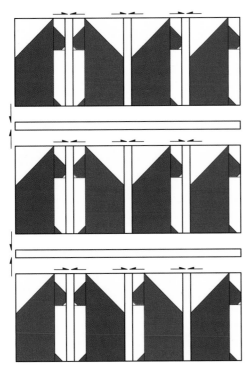

Press all seams toward the sashing.

Adding Borders

All the quilts in this book have simple, straight-cut borders. Add the border strips to opposite sides of the quilt and press the seam allowances toward the border. Then add the remaining two border strips.

Although exact measurements for straight-cut borders are provided in the project cutting directions, measure your quilt first and cut the border strips to fit. Measure the width and length in two or three places toward the center of the quilt rather than along the edges, since the edges tend to stretch out of shape. Use an average of these measurements for the cut length of the strips to ensure a "square" quilt when you are finished.

I prefer to cut outer borders parallel to the selvages because the fabric stretches less along the lengthwise grain than it does along the crosswise grain. To avoid piecing the border strips, I usually buy enough fabric to allow for cutting the longest border. For example, if the longest border is 50", I purchase at least 54" (1½ yards) to allow for shrinkage.

If borders are no wider than 7", you'll have enough border fabric to cut binding strips as well. If you plan to use a different fabric for the binding, you'll have fabric left over for another project.

If you prefer to purchase less fabric, you can cut border strips along the crosswise grain and piece them to the required length. In the quiltmaking directions, yardage requirements are provided for both methods whenever cutting crosswise would require less fabric.

Finishing the Quilt

You are ready to complete your quilt project by adding batting and backing and quilting the layers together. Binding is the final step. Some quilts in this book also require embroidered details.

Preparing the Backing

Usually the backing for a small quilt can be cut from the width of the fabric. Be sure to trim off the selvages, which can draw in the edges and prevent the back from lying flat.

For quilts over 40" wide, you will need to piece the backing, unless you can find a suitable 90"-wide backing fabric. For quilts up to 80" wide, simply piece two lengths of fabric together with a long center seam. For a quilt 50" to 60" wide, use one length of fabric, and then make it large enough by adding a matching or contrasting fabric strip or a strip of pieced blocks or scraps to one side to make the backing large enough. Be creative!

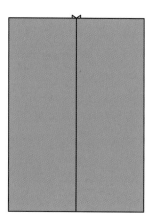

For quilts up to 80" wide.

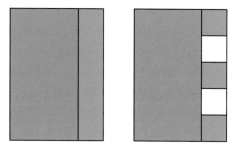

For quilts 50" to 60" wide.

Making the Quilt Sandwich

When the quilt top is complete and the backing is ready, you will sandwich a piece of batting between the two layers and baste them all together for the quilting process. Purchase packaged batting intended for hand or machine quilting. Remove it from the package the night before you want to use it to allow it to relax. You can steam out any wrinkles with a steam iron held slightly above the batting.

1. Lay the quilt backing, wrong side up, on the floor or other large, flat surface. Smooth out all wrinkles. Use masking tape around the edges to hold the backing in place.

2. Lay the batting on top of the quilt backing and smooth out any wrinkles.

3. Smooth the quilt top over the batting, right side up, and pin through all the layers around the edges.

4. Using white thread, hand baste the layers together with 1"-long stitches, in horizontal and vertical lines spaced about 3" apart. Also baste ¼" from the outer edges. Remove the pins.

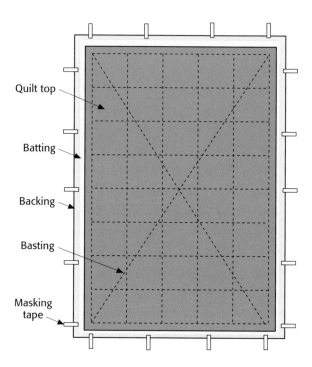

Quilt top

Batting

Backing

Basting

Masking
tape

Quilting

Quilting stitches hold the layers of the quilt sandwich together and can be done by hand or by machine—it's your choice.

Hand quilting is simply a short running stitch. Work with a relatively short length of thread, no more than 18" long, and bury all knots inside the quilt in the batting. Use short quilting needles called *betweens* to make it easier to take small stitches.

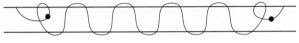

Be sure stitches go through all three layers.

If you prefer to quilt by machine, set the stitch for a slightly longer length than you normally use for stitching the seams. Roll up the parts of the quilt you aren't working on to keep them out of the way. Whenever possible, start and stop stitching at the edges of the quilt so the thread ends will be covered by the binding. You also won't have to tie off the thread ends—a tedious job at best.

Binding

Finish the edges of your quilt with binding after completing all the quilting. I recommend a binding that finishes to ½" and is cut from straight-grain strips.

1. Cut 2¾"-wide, straight-grain strips from the binding fabric. Cut enough strips to go around the quilt, plus about 20" extra for joining the strips and turning the corners.

2. Join the strips at right angles with a diagonal seam as shown. Trim away the excess, leaving a ¼"-wide seam allowance. Press the seams open to eliminate lumps in the finished binding.

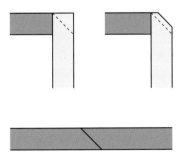

3. Trim one end of the strip at a 45° angle and press under ¼". Fold the strip in half lengthwise, wrong sides together, and press.

4. *Trim the batting and backing* so that they extend ¼" beyond the raw edge of the quilt top.

5. With right sides together and the binding raw edges even with the quilt-top edge (not the batting and backing edge), machine stitch the binding to the quilt ¼" from the quilt-top edge.

6. Stop stitching ¼" from the edge of the quilt top (½" from the edge of the batting and backing) and backstitch.

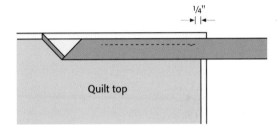

Quilt top

7. At the corner, fold the binding strip away from you and then back toward you as shown, lining up the fold with the top edges of the batting and backing, and aligning the raw edges of the binding with the edge of the quilt top. Start sewing at the fold, backstitch, and then continue to the next corner.

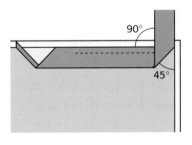

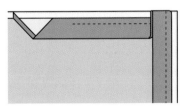

8. Repeat steps 5–7 to complete the remaining sides and corners.

9. End by overlapping the diagonally cut end by 1". Trim the excess strip parallel to the diagonal end. Tack the end into the beginning of the binding and complete the stitching.

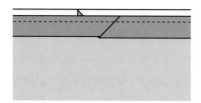

Tuck end into beginning of binding and complete stitching.

10. Fold the binding to the back of the quilt and hand stitch in place. A miter will form at each corner on the front of the quilt. Fold the binding to create the miter on the back side of the quilt.

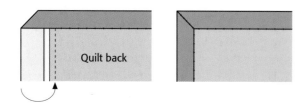

Quilt back

Adding Details

Cats and dogs need eyes and noses, and these can be embroidered using two or three strands of embroidery floss.

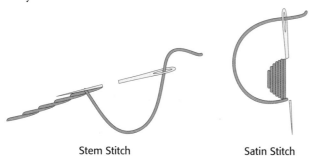

Stem Stitch   Satin Stitch

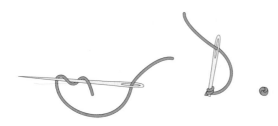

French Knot

Use a satin stitch for eyes. Take up-and-down stitches rather than side-to-side ones.

If you prefer, you can use synthetic suede, such as Ultra Suede, for larger appliquéd features such as dogs' noses. Cut the shapes without a turn-under allowance and sew in place with the appliqué stitch described on pages 11–12. It isn't necessary to turn under the edges of nonwoven or knit synthetic suede, so you don't need to add a turn-under allowance when cutting shapes from the suede. Synthetic suede is washable, but it is also heat-sensitive, so be careful with the iron temperature when pressing finished blocks. For projects that won't be laundered, you can use felt in place of synthetic suede.

Beads also make good eyes. Sew them in place after the quilt is completed, sewing through all layers for added security. If you use buttons for eyes, be sure to use small ones—otherwise they look like goggles.

Fabric paint is a fast alternative to embroidery. I like the fabric paint that comes in little squeeze bottles because it's thick enough to make a round, shiny dot for an eye.

Cat Chat

Embroidery and Machine Quilting

If you plan to have your project machine quilted in an overall design, add the eyes and noses after the machine quilting is completed so that they will stand out on the quilt surface.

Christmas Cat Chat

*These speed-pieced cats in Christmas colors seem to be chatting, nose to nose.
I wonder what their holiday gossip is all about! If red and green don't suit
your fancy, choose your favorite holiday colors for these friendly felines.*

58" x 73", by Torch Area Artisans Guild; quilted by Nancy Webster

Finished Quilt: 58" x 73"
Finished Block: 6½" x 11"

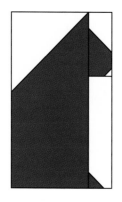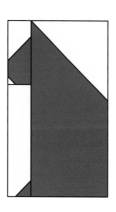

Cutting

Cats

Cut 30 cats, 3 each from 10 different fabrics.

Piece	No. of Pieces	Dimensions
A	3	5½" x 11½"
B	3	2" x 3½"
C	3	1½" x 1½"

Background, Inner Border, and Sashing

Cut the inner border and sashing pieces first, parallel to the selvages, and then cut cat background pieces from the remaining fabric.

Piece	No. of Pieces	Dimensions
Side borders	2	1½" x 59½"
Top and bottom borders	2	1½" x 44½"
Horizontal sashing	4	1½" x 46½"
Vertical sashing	25	1½" x 11½"
D (cats)	30	5½" x 5½"
E (cats)	30	2" x 7½"
F (cats)	30	2" x 3"
G (cats)	30	1" x 1"

Outer Border and Binding

Piece	No. of Pieces	Dimensions
Side borders	2	6½" x 61½"
Top and bottom borders	2	6½" x 58½"
Binding	7	2¾" x 40"

Materials

Yardage is based on 42"-wide fabric, with 40" of usable width after preshrinking.

¼ yd. or 1 fat quarter each of 5 different red and 5 different green fabrics for cats

2½ yds. light fabric for block backgrounds, inner border, and sashing

2 yds. red-and-green print for outer border*

3¾ yds. for backing

¾ yd. red print for binding

59" x 74" piece of batting

*Borders are cut from the fabric length to avoid piecing; you will have excess fabric to add to your fabric collection. If you prefer no excess, purchase 1½ yards, cut strips across the fabric width, and piece the strips as needed.

Making the Blocks

Referring to "Flip-and-Sew Piecing" on pages 9–10 and the illustrations below, make 30 Cat blocks, 3 from each of the 10 cat fabrics. Make 15 right-facing and 15 left-facing Cat blocks.

1. Sew D to A; trim and press as shown to make body unit A/D.

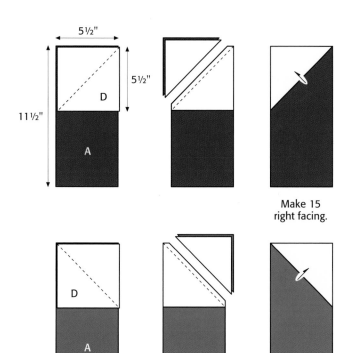

2. Sew C to background E; trim and press as shown.

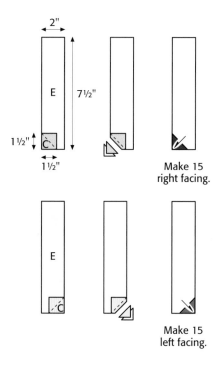

3. Sew background F to head B; trim and press as shown. Add a background G to the lower corner of B as shown.

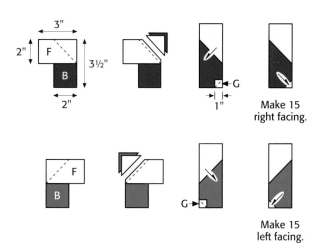

4. Sew each B/G/F head unit to the C/E background unit. Add the resulting unit to the A/D body unit.

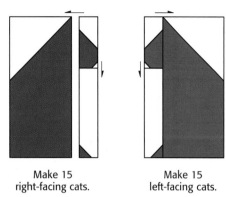

Make 15
right-facing cats.

Make 15
left-facing cats.

Assembling the Quilt Top

1. Referring to the quilt plan below, arrange and sew the Cat blocks together in 5 horizontal rows of 6 blocks each, with a 1½" x 11½" sashing strip between each pair of cats. Press all seams toward the sashing.

2. Sew the rows together with 1½" x 44½" sashing strips between the rows. Press all seams toward the sashing.

3. Referring to "Adding Borders" on page 13, sew the side inner borders to the quilt top and press the seams toward the borders. Add the top and bottom inner borders and press.

4. Add the side outer borders, followed by the top and bottom outer borders. Press all seams toward the inner border.

Finishing

Refer to "Finishing the Quilt" on pages 14–16.

1. Layer the quilt top with batting and backing, and then baste the layers together.

2. Hand or machine quilt as desired.

3. Bind the edges and add a label to the back if you desire.

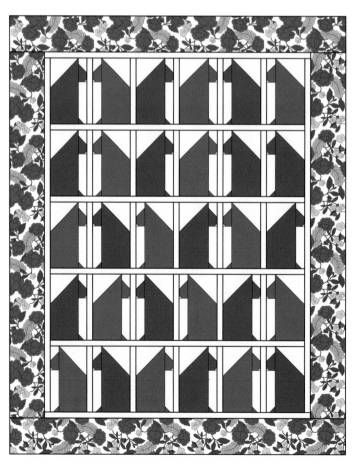

Quilt Plan

Snowcats

Look twice and you'll see that these snowmen have cat ears—all the better to hear the snowmice scurrying in the sashing. The cats wear perky bowties and pretty buttons all in a row.

28" x 32", by Janet Kime

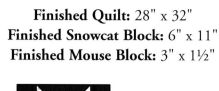

Finished Quilt: 28" x 32"
Finished Snowcat Block: 6" x 11"
Finished Mouse Block: 3" x 1½"

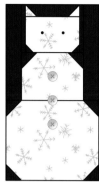

Snowcat Block    Mouse Block

Materials

Yardage is based on 42"-wide fabric, with 40" of usable width after preshrinking.

6 different 9" x 14" light print scraps (or 6 different fat quarters) for snowcats

10 different 2" x 5" light print scraps for mice

3 different 2" x 5½" scraps for bowties

1¼ yds. dark print for background and binding

1 yd. for backing

29" x 33" piece of batting

1 skein each of brown and white embroidery floss

12 black beads, ⅛" diameter, for cats' eyes

18 assorted buttons (6 sets of 3), ½" to 1" diameter, for cats' buttons

Cutting

Snowcats
Cut 6, each from a different fabric.

Piece	No. of Pieces	Dimensions
A	1	2¾" x 4"
B	2	1¼" x 1¼"
C	1	3½" x 4½"
D	1	5½" x 6½"

Bowties
Cut 3, each from a different fabric.

Piece	No. of Pieces	Dimensions
JJ	1	2" x 4"
KK	1	¾" x 1"

Mice
Cut 10, each from a different fabric.

Piece	No. of Pieces	Dimensions
J	1	2" x 3½"
Template K	2	

Snowcats and Mice Background

Piece	No. of Pieces	Dimensions
E (cats)	12	1" x 1"
F (cats)	6	1¼" x 4"
G (cats)	12	¾" x 3½"
H (cats)	36	1½" x 1½"
I (cats)	12	1½" x 6½"
L (mice)	20	2" x 2"
M (mice)	20	1⅛" x 2"
N (mice)	6	1" x 3½"

Background and Binding

Stack the following pieces in order as you cut them.

Piece	No. of Pieces	Dimensions
O	1	1½" x 11½"
P	1	1½" x 7½"
Q	1	2½" x 7½"
R	1	2" x 6½"
S	1	2" x 3½"
T	1	1½" x 14½"
U	2	2½" x 11½"
V	1	1½" x 11½"
W	1	2½" x 7½"
X	1	3½" x 7½"
Y	1	1½" x 3½"
Z	1	1½" x 3"
AA	1	3" x 4½"
CC	1	2½" x 3½"
BB	1	2" x 3½"
DD	1	3½" x 4"
EE	2	1½" x 6½"
FF	2	3" x 12½"
GG	2	2½" x 28½"
HH	2	2½" x 15½"
II	2	2½" x 4½"
Binding	4	2¾" x 40"

Making the Snowcat Blocks

Referring to "Flip-and-Sew Piecing" on pages 9–10 and the illustrations below, make 6 Snowcat blocks.

1. Sew background E to the lower corners of each snowcat head A. Press.

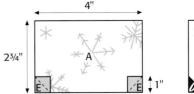

2. Sew ear squares B to opposite ends of each background F. Press.

3. Sew ears unit to the top edge of the snowcat head. Press the seam toward the head.

4. Add background G to opposite sides of the head. Trim the seam allowances to ⅛" and press toward the background strips.

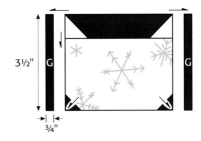

5. Sew 2 background H to snowcat upper body C. Trim and press.

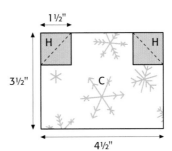
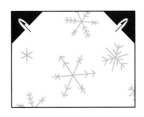

6. Sew the upper body unit to the lower edge of the head unit. Press toward the upper body. Add background I to the resulting head/body unit. Press as directed.

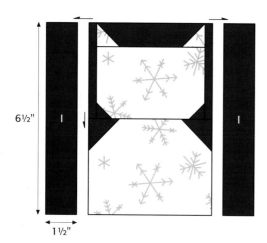

7. Sew a background H to each corner of the snowcat lower body D. Press.

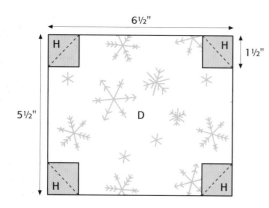

8. Sew the resulting unit to the lower edge of the head/upper-body unit and press the seam toward the upper body.

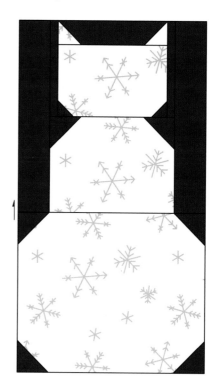

Making the Mouse Blocks

Referring to the directions for "Flip-and-Sew Piecing" on pages 9–10 and the illustrations below, make 10 Mouse blocks.

1. Sew a background L to opposite upper corners of each mouse body J. Trim and press.

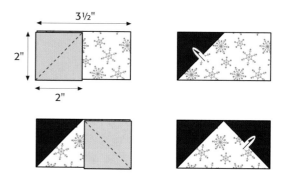

2. Trim ⅝" from both short edges of each mouse unit.

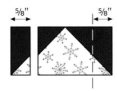

3. Add a background M to each trimmed edge of the mouse unit from step 2. Press toward the background strip. Referring to "Adding Appliqués" on pages 11–12 and using template K below, prepare the mouse ears. Position as shown in the block diagram and sew in place.

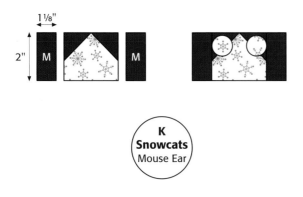

K
Snowcats
Mouse Ear

4. Add a background N to the upper edge of 6 of the Mouse blocks from step 3; press. Set aside for the top and bottom borders.

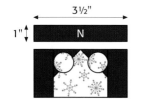

Make 6 border units.

Assembling the Quilt Top

1. Referring to the photo on page 21, arrange the snowcats and mice with the remaining pieces of the quilt.

2. Assemble the quilt top, section by section as shown on this and the following page. Use the background pieces in order, beginning with piece O. Press seams in the direction of the arrows in each section.

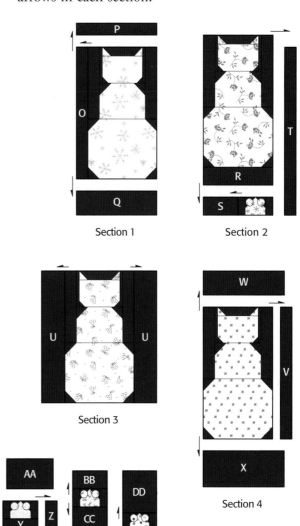

Section 1

Section 2

Section 3

Section 4

Section 5

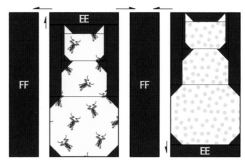

Section 6

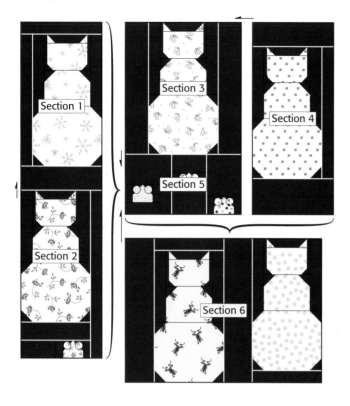

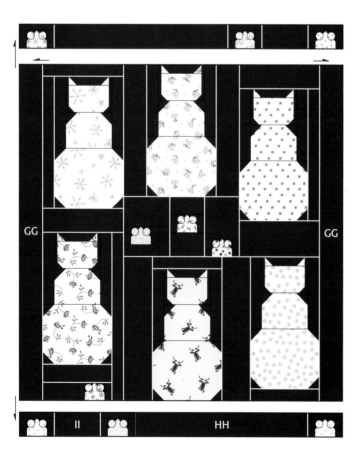

3. Using 3 strands of brown embroidery floss, embroider the snowcat arms and hands with 2 side-by-side rows of stem stitching (see "Adding Details" on page 16).

Do two side-by-side rows of stem stitches for snowcats' arms and hands.

4. Draw the mice tails freehand, referring to the photograph on page 21. Embroider with white floss, referring to the tip box on page 27.

Finishing

Refer to "Finishing the Quilt" on pages 14–16.

1. Layer the quilt top with batting and backing, and then baste the layers together.
2. Machine or hand quilt freehand curls of wind between the cats and in the border. Do not remove the basting.
3. Sew on bead eyes and buttons, sewing through all layers. Remove the basting.
4. For each bowtie, fold JJ in half lengthwise, right sides together, and stitch ¼" from the long raw edges. Turn right side out and finger-press with the seam running down the center on the underside of the strip. Fold the 2 short ends to the center over the seam line and tack in place with small hand stitches.

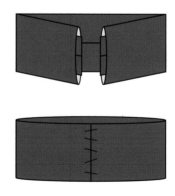

5. Accordion-pleat the bow 2 or 3 times in the center; stitch through the folds a few times to hold them in place. Fasten off with a few stitches in place.

6. Fold under the long edges of piece KK, overlapping them. Wrap around the pleated center of the bow and hand tack the raw edges together on the back of the bow.

7. Sew a bow to 3 snowcats, just below the seam that joins the head to the body.

8. Bind the quilt and add a label.

Cat Chat

Novelty Embroidery

This easy, decorative stitch looks like tiny rickrack. Start and stop the stitching where the tail emerges from the mouse body, hiding your knot in the mouse seam allowances.

1. Starting at the mouse body, embroider the tail with a simple running stitch.

2. At the tip of the tail, start back in the other direction, weaving the needle and thread through the stitches on top of the quilt. Fasten off with a few backstitches in the mouse seam allowances.

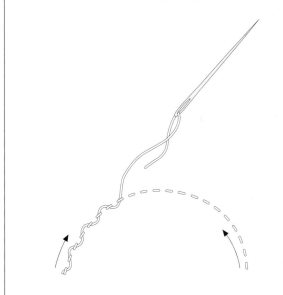

Christmas Stockings

These Christmas stockings are quick and easy to sew. Make several large and medium-size ones to use around your house and fill them with evergreen branches or wrapped packages. The smaller, ornament-size stockings are great for package decorations. I used Christmas flannels for my stockings, but you could use cotton, corduroy, or even polar fleece for a similar, homey effect. For a sumptuous look, try satin, brocade, velvet, or metallic fabric.

Christmas Stockings
in various sizes
by Janet Kime

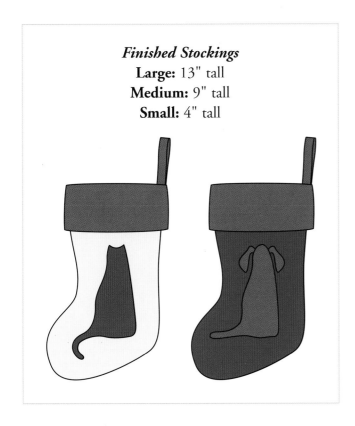

Finished Stockings
Large: 13" tall
Medium: 9" tall
Small: 4" tall

Materials

Yardage is based on 42"-wide fabric, with 40" of usable width after preshrinking.

	Large	Medium	Small
Stocking	⅓ yd. or 1 fat quarter	¼ yd. or 1 fat quarter	Fabric scraps
Cuff	⅓ yd. or 1 fat quarter	¼ yd. or 1 fat quarter	Fabric scraps
Appliqués	Fabric scraps	Fabric scraps	Fabric scraps
			Scrap of fusible web
			Perle cotton or other strong thread

Cutting

Use the stocking templates on pages 32–36.

Large

Piece	No. of Pieces	Dimensions
Stocking	1 + 1 reversed	
Cuff	1	10½" x 16"
Hanging loop	1	2" x 7"*

Medium

Piece	No. of Pieces	Dimensions
Stocking	1 + 1 reversed	
Cuff	1	8" x 12"
Hanging loop	1	1½" x 6"*

Small

Piece	No. of Pieces	Dimensions
Stocking	1 + 1 reversed	
Cuff	1	4" x 5½"
Hanging loop	1	6"-long piece of perle cotton

Cut the fabric strips for hanging loops with one short end on the selvage.

Dog Talk

Sewing with Flannel

If you are using flannel for the stocking, do not prewash. Flannel has more body and is easier to work with *before* it has been washed, and since the finished projects will not be washed, shrinkage is not an issue.

Making the Stocking

1. Referring to "Adding Appliqués" on pages 11–12, prepare the cat or dog appliqués. Arrange and sew the appliqués to 1 of the 2 stocking pieces. For the small stocking size, use fusible web to apply the appliqués instead of turning under the edges and stitching. Back the appliqué fabric scraps with fusible web and trace the patterns onto the transfer-paper backing. Cut out on the drawn lines and fuse to the stocking, following the manufacturer's directions.

2. With right sides facing, stitch the 2 stocking pieces together from A to B. Use a ¼"-wide seam allowance and finger-press the seam open.

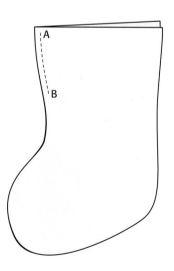

3. Turn under and press ¼" on one long edge of the cuff. With your machine set for a basting-length stitch, sew ¼" from the remaining long edge of the cuff. Leaving the thread tails free at the end where you started, backstitch to end the stitching.

4. With right sides together, pin the stitched edge of the cuff to the upper edge of the stocking and draw up the stitching to fit. Adjust gathers evenly around the cuff. Stitch ¼" from the raw edges and finger-press the seam allowances toward the cuff.

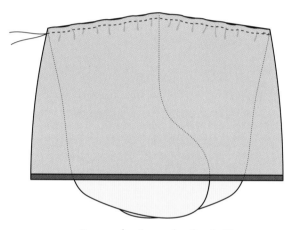

Draw up basting and gather to fit.

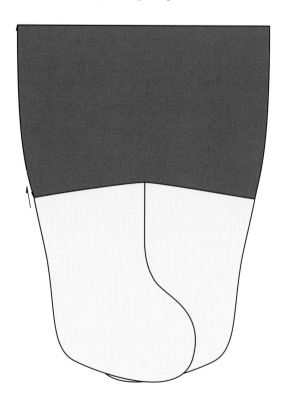

Cat Chat

Embroidered Stockings

Rather than appliqué the cat and dog, you might prefer to embroider the designs with a stem stitch. This works especially well for the small stocking.

5. With the stocking and cuff right sides together, stitch the remainder of the seam. Begin at B and end at the upper raw edge of the cuff. Clip the inner curve.

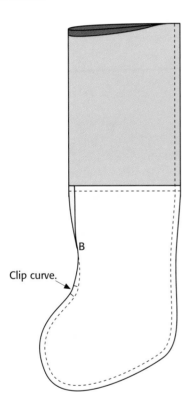

B

Clip curve.

6. Turn the cuff down over the seam allowance, with the folded edge along the stitching, and hand sew in place, easing in the extra fullness as you go. The fullness in the cuff allows the cuff room to fit comfortably when turned down over the right side of the completed stocking.

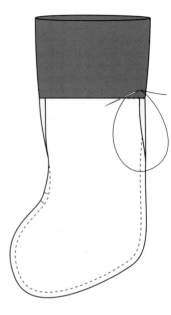

7. Turn the stocking right side out and fold the cuff down over the stocking so the lower edge covers the upper seam. Finger-press the outer edges of the stocking flat.

8. Fold the loop strip in half lengthwise with right sides together. Stitch ¼" from the long raw edges and turn right side out. Tack to the inside of the stocking at the back edge, with the short selvage end over the short raw edge to cover it. For the small stocking, make a hanging loop from a 6"-long piece of perle cotton and sew in place.

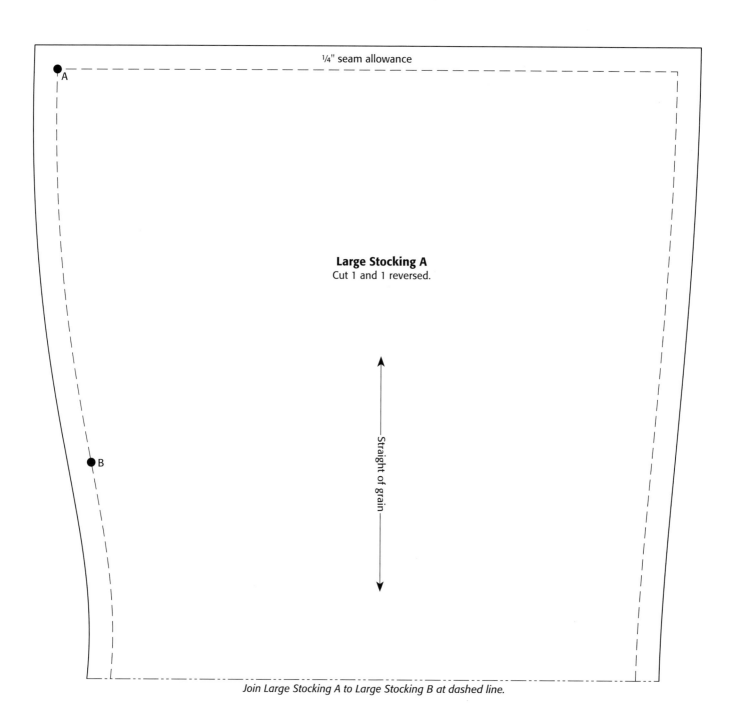

¼" seam allowance

A

Large Stocking A
Cut 1 and 1 reversed.

Straight of grain

B

Join Large Stocking A to Large Stocking B at dashed line.

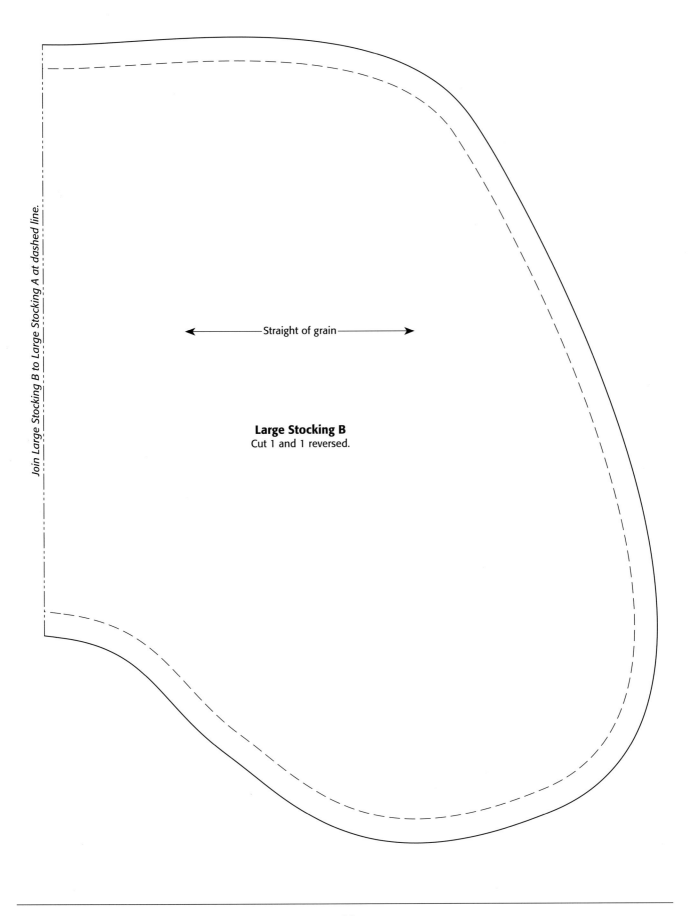

Join Large Stocking B to Large Stocking A at dashed line.

←——— Straight of grain ———→

Large Stocking B
Cut 1 and 1 reversed.

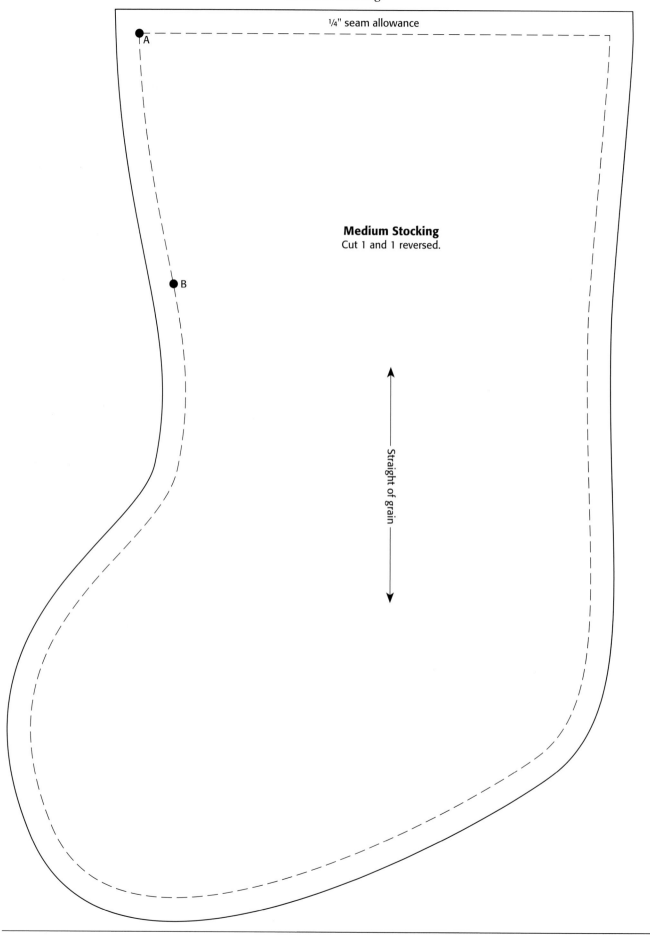

¼" seam allowance

A

B

Medium Stocking
Cut 1 and 1 reversed.

Straight of grain

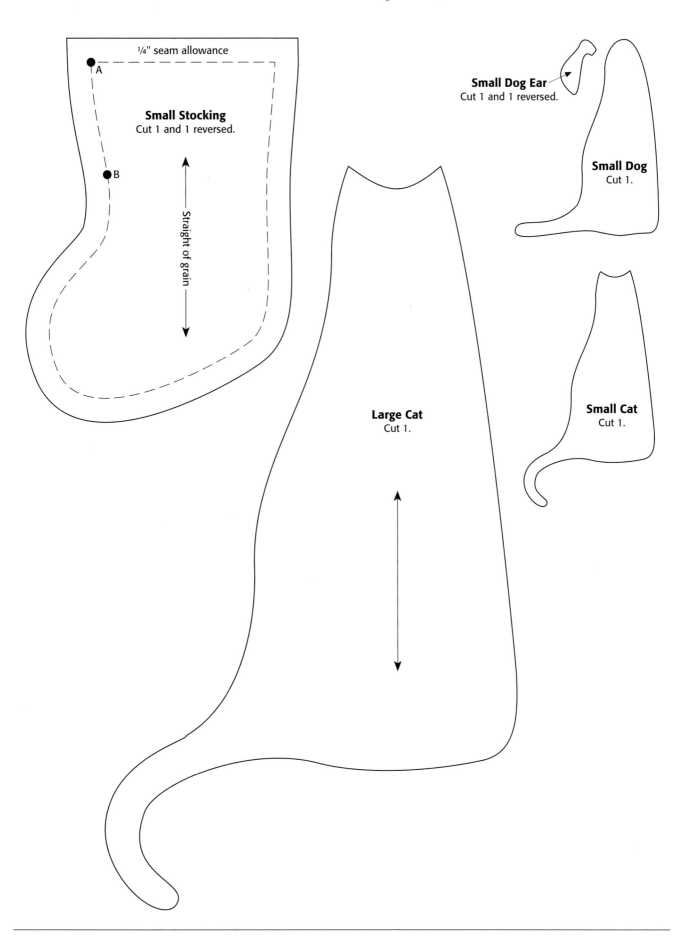

¼" seam allowance

A

Small Stocking
Cut 1 and 1 reversed.

B

Straight of grain

Small Dog Ear
Cut 1 and 1 reversed.

Small Dog
Cut 1.

Large Cat
Cut 1.

Small Cat
Cut 1.

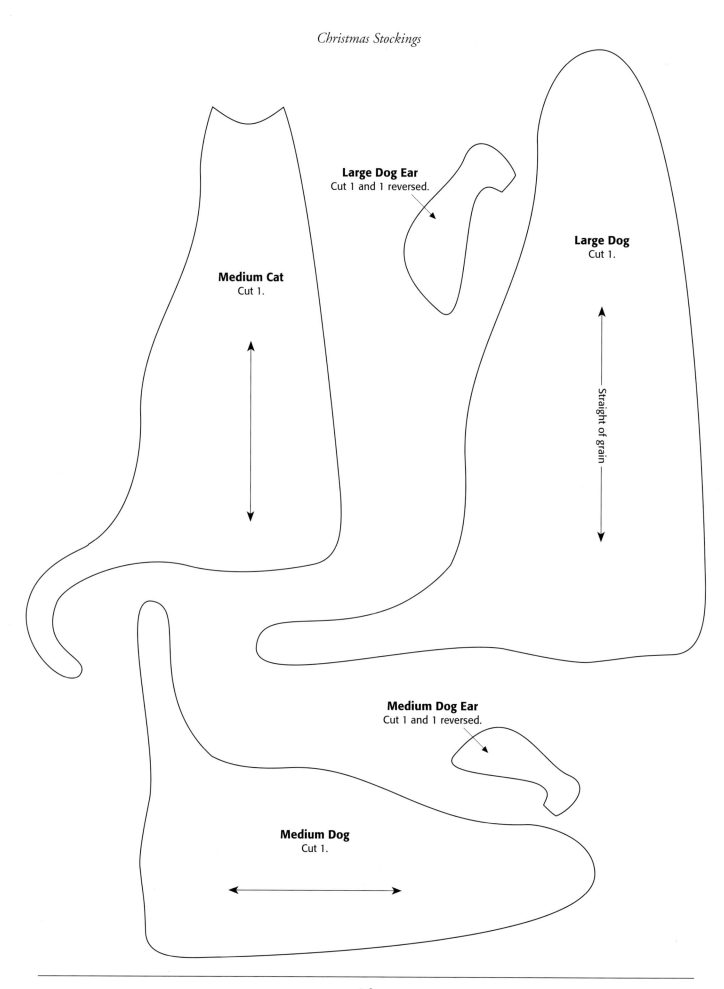

Large Dog Ear
Cut 1 and 1 reversed.

Medium Cat
Cut 1.

Large Dog
Cut 1.

Straight of grain

Medium Dog Ear
Cut 1 and 1 reversed.

Medium Dog
Cut 1.

Peace on Earth

These stately angels with their sparkling star halos are easy to appliqué.
This heavenly quilt is a good project for beginners.

30" x 39", by Carolyn Bohot

Finished Quilt: 30" x 39"
Finished Block: 6" x 9"

Materials

Yardage is based on 42"-wide fabric, with 40" of usable width after preshrinking.

Assorted fabric scraps for angels

1 yd. tone-on-tone light print for block backgrounds and inner border

⅓ yd. blue print for stars

1 yd. print for border and binding

1 yd. fabric for backing

31" x 40" piece of batting

Black embroidery floss

Small sequin stars for halos

Brass seed beads for halos

Cutting

See "Making the Blocks and Border Units" on page 39 for cutting the angel appliqués.

Star

Piece	No. of Pieces	Dimensions
	64	1½" x 4"

Background and Inner Border

Piece	No. of Pieces	Dimensions
Angel blocks	9	7" x 10"
Side border blocks	6	3½" x 9½"
Top and bottom border blocks	6	3½" x 6½"
Corner border blocks	4	3½" x 3½"

Outer Border and Binding
Cut strips parallel to the selvages.

Piece	No. of Pieces	Dimensions
Side borders	2	3½" x 33½"
Top and bottom borders	2	3½" x 30½"
Binding	5	2¾" x 36"

Making the Blocks and Border Units

Use the templates on page 43.

1. Referring to "Adding Appliqués" on pages 11–12, cut the angel appliqué pieces from assorted prints for 9 different blocks. Prepare the pieces for appliqué using the paper-patch method. Do not turn under the top edge of cat body B and the bottom edges of ears C and D. Press the prepared pieces.

2. Referring to the placement diagram on page 43, position and stitch the appliqués to each 7" x 10" background piece. Match the cross in cat body B to the center of the background fabric piece. Appliqué wings A first, then cat body B, then ears C and D. Place the larger ear C on the left on some cats and on the right on others. Appliqué the cat head E last, covering the open edges of the ears and body.

3. Embroider French knots for the cats' eyes, using 2 strands of black embroidery floss.

4. Press the completed blocks and trim each block to 6½" x 9½", centering the angel in each.

5. With the cat upright in each block, make a mark on the edge of the block ¾" from the upper right corner. Make another mark 2½" below the upper right corner.

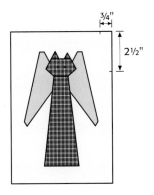

6. Rotate the block 90° and mark the bottom right corner in the same manner.

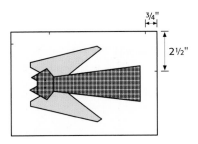

7. Rotate the block and mark the remaining corners in the same manner.

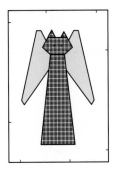

8. In the same manner, mark 2 corners at opposite ends of the 3½" x 9½" background pieces. Repeat with the 3½" x 6½" background pieces. Mark 1 corner of each 3½" background square.

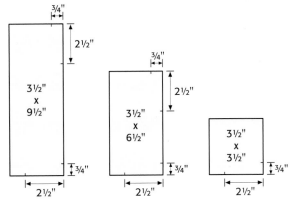

Mark 2 corners.   Mark 1 corner.

9. With right sides together, position a blue star piece at the upper right corner, aligning the edges of the piece with the marks on the block. Pin in place and stitch ¼" from the raw edge of the star piece.

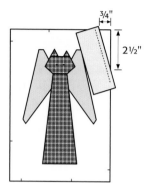

10. Flip the star piece over the seam and press. Trim the star fabric even with the edges of the block.

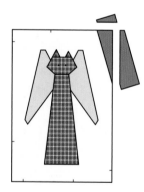

11. Repeat steps 9 and 10 on the remaining 3 corners of each Angel block.

Make 9.

12. Add star points to each of the marked corners on the background pieces in the same manner.

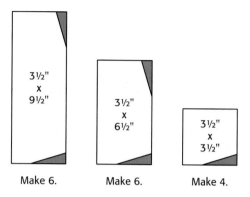

Make 6. Make 6. Make 4.

Assembling the Quilt Top

1. Referring to the photo on page 37, arrange the blocks and longest border units in 3 horizontal rows and sew together. Press the seams in opposite directions from row to row.

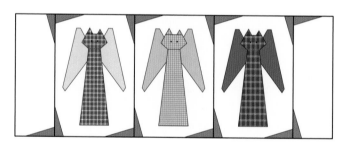

Make 3 rows.
Press seams in opposite directions from row to row.

2. Using the remaining border units, make the top and bottom inner borders and add to the quilt. Press the seams in opposite directions from the seams in the block rows.

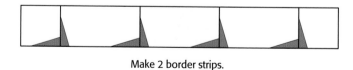

Make 2 border strips.

3. Referring to "Adding Borders" on page 13, add the side outer borders, followed by the top and bottom outer borders. Press all seams toward the outer borders.

Finishing

Refer to "Finishing the Quilt" on pages 14–16.

1. Layer the quilt top with batting and backing, and then baste the layers together.
2. Quilt around each cat and star and in-the-ditch along the outer border seams.

3. To create an arc of stars above each cat for a halo, refer to the placement diagram on page 43 and use a seed bead to hold each star sequin in place.

4. Bind the quilt and add a label.

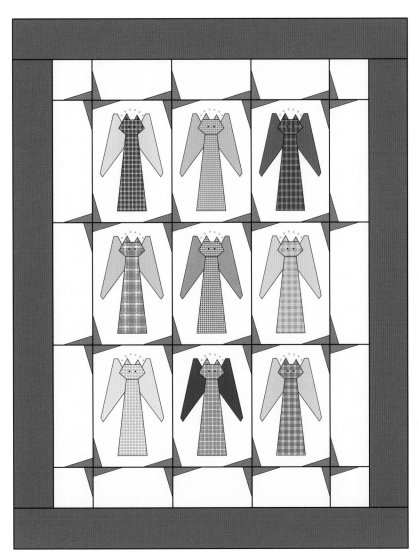

Quilt Plan

Angel Ornament

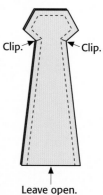

Use the templates on page 43.

In addition to fabric scraps, you will need a small piece of lightweight fusible interfacing for the wings of each ornament, a handful of polyester fiberfill for stuffing, a 1¼"-diameter gold hoop earring finding for the halo, a large needle, and white glue. Use clear nylon thread for the hanging loop.

1. Trace the cat head and body templates and tape together at the neck to make one template.

2. With the fabric pieces for the cat body, cat wings, and ears each placed right sides together, trace around the template on the wrong side of one of the fabric pieces for each one.

3. Sew the ear pieces on the drawn lines, leaving the bottom edges open. Trim away the excess fabric, leaving an ⅛"-wide allowance all around. Turn the ears right side out.

4. Cut out the cat pieces ¼" outside the drawn lines. Pin the ears to the right side of a cat head, with the ears pointing down and the raw edges of the ears overlapping the upper drawn line by ⅛".

5. With right sides together, place the remaining cat piece on top. Stitch ¼" from the raw edges, leaving the bottom edge unstitched.

Clip the corners to eliminate bulk. Turn right side out, stuff lightly with fiberfill, and slipstitch the opening closed. Embroider French knots for the eyes, using 2 strands of embroidery floss.

Clip.   Clip.

Leave open.

6. Trace around the wing template on 2 pieces of fusible interfacing and cut out ⅛" *inside* the drawn line. Fuse to the wrong side of 1 piece of each of the sets of wing pieces (4 pieces per angel).

7. With right sides together, stitch each interfaced wing to a noninterfaced one, leaving a 2" opening for turning. Turn right side out and slipstitch the openings closed. Press. Tack the wings to the back of the cat body.

8. To make the halo, use wire clippers or an old pair of scissors to clip the fastener from a 1¼" gold hoop earring finding. Poke holes on both sides of the cat's head with a large needle, put a drop of white glue in each, and insert the ends of the hoop in the holes. Hang the ornament from a loop of clear nylon thread.

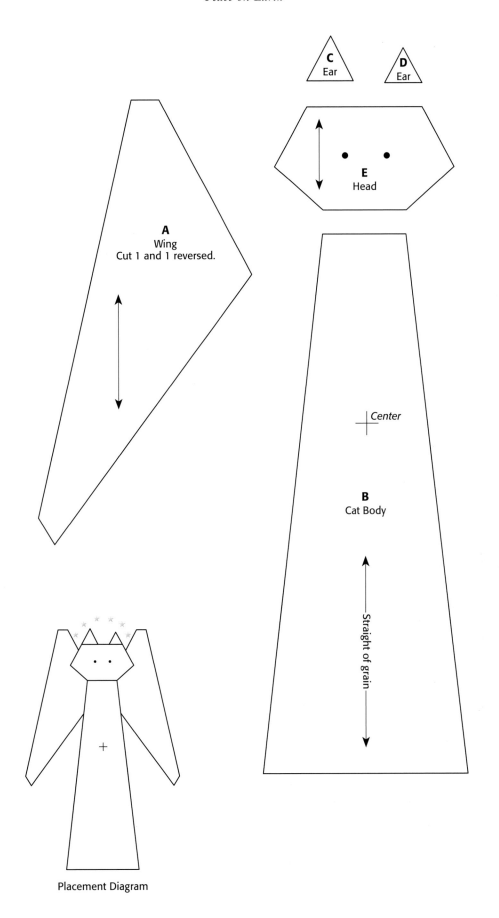

C
Ear

D
Ear

E
Head

A
Wing
Cut 1 and 1 reversed.

Center

B
Cat Body

Straight of grain

Placement Diagram

Santadogs

*These pooches are all dressed up as Santa Claus (Santa Claws?) for the holidays.
Make your blocks as scrappy as the sample quilt, or if you prefer, use only one
background fabric and choose dog colors for the Santas.*

65" x 81", by Janet Kime; quilted by Nancy Weed

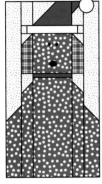

Finished Quilt: 65" x 81"
Finished Santadog Block: 6" x 11"
Finished Sawtooth Star Block: 6" square

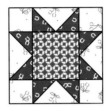

Santadog Block   Sawtooth Star Block

Materials

Yardage is based on 42"-wide fabric, with 40" of usable width after preshrinking.

1½ yds. *total* assorted red prints for Santadog blocks

⅛ yd. muslin or light tone-on-tone prints for hat brims and pompons

3½ yds. *total* assorted light prints for block backgrounds and inner border

1½ yds. *total* assorted red prints for stars

2¼ yds. red print for outer border and binding

5 yds. for backing

66" x 82" piece of batting

Black embroidery floss

Optional: Ultra Suede for appliqués

Cutting

To keep them in order, put all the pieces for each Santadog and each Star in its own self-sealing plastic bag.

Santadogs

Cut 18 Santadogs, each from a set of 4 fabrics—one each for the dog body, dog ear, hat brim/pompon, and hat/collar.

Dog body

Piece	No. of Pieces	Dimensions
A	1	3" x 3"
K	1	3" x 6¾"
L	2	1¼" x 6½"
N	2	1½" x 5"

Dog ear

Piece	No. of Pieces	Dimensions
B	2	1¼" x 3"

Brim/pompon

Piece	No. of Pieces	Dimensions
D	1	1" x 3¾"
Template P	1	

Hat/collar

Piece	No. of Pieces	Dimensions
E	1	2" x 3"
I	1	1¼" x 1¼"
J	1	¾" x 3"
Q	1	2" x 4"
R	1	¾" x 1"

Dog Talk

Scrap Quilts

It takes longer to cut out the pieces for a scrap quilt than for a quilt that requires only a few different fabrics. Just preparing a few dozen fabrics for rotary cutting takes a lot of time. In a quilt such as "Santadogs," where each block requires five fabrics that must contrast with one another, it also takes time to plan the fabric combinations. To speed things up when cutting the pieces for a large quilt with many blocks, cut two or three duplicates of each fabric combination. In "Santadogs," for example, there are nine matched pairs of Santadog blocks.

Stars

Cut 34 stars, each from a set of 2 fabrics—one for the star points and one for the star center.

Points

Piece	No. of Pieces	Dimensions
T	8	2" x 2"

Center

Piece	No. of Pieces	Dimensions
W	1	3½" x 3½"

Stars Background
Cut 34 sets.

Piece	No. of Pieces	Dimensions
U	4	2" x 3½"
V	4	2" x 2"

Santadogs Background
Cut 18 sets.

Piece	No. of Pieces	Dimensions
C	2	1¼" x 1¼"
F	2	⅞" x 1"
G	1	2" x 2"
H	2	1¼" x 2"
M	2	1¼" x 1¾"
O	2	1½" x 8"

Assembly Pieces and Inner Border
Cut X, Y, and the vertical sashing pieces from several different background fabrics.

Piece	No. of Pieces	Dimensions
X	52	1½" x 6½"
Y	18	2½" x 6½"
Vertical sashing	30	2" x 14½"
Side borders	2	2½" x 70½"
Top and bottom borders	2	2" x 55½"

Outer Border and Binding
Cut all strips parallel to the selvages.

Piece	No. of Pieces	Dimensions
Side borders	2	5½" x 73½"
Top and bottom borders	2	4½" x 65½"
Binding	4	2¾" x 81"

Making the Santadog Blocks

Referring to "Flip-and-Sew Piecing" on pages 9–10 and the illustrations below, make 18 Santadog blocks.

1. Sew a background C to one short end of ear B. Make 1 and 1 reversed. Trim and press.

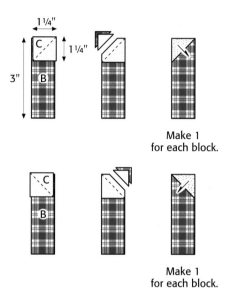

Make 1
for each block.

Make 1
for each block.

2. Sew ear units from step 1 to opposite sides of 3" x 3" head A. Press the seams toward the face.

3. Sew a background F to each short end of hat brim D. Sew to the top edge of the head unit. Press.

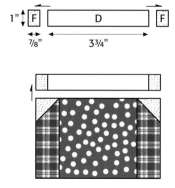

4. Sew background G to hat piece E and add background H to G. Press.

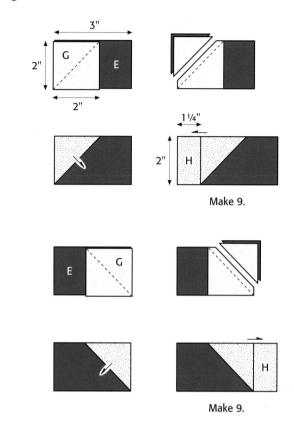

Make 9.

Make 9.

5. Sew hat point I to one end of a second background H. Sew the resulting H/I unit to the opposite end of the hat unit. For variety, make 9 hats with the tip pointing right and 9 hats with the tip pointing left.

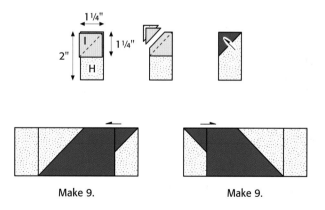

Make 9.   Make 9.

6. Sew the hat unit to the upper edge of the hat brim, completing the head unit. Press toward the brim.

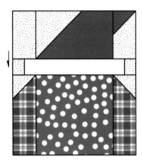

7. Sew collar J to the top edge of each dog body K. Press toward the collar.

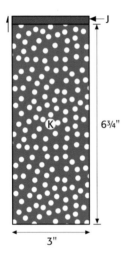

8. Sew background M to the end of front leg L. Press. Make 1 and 1 reversed.

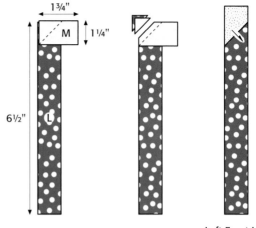

Left Front Leg
Make 1 for each block.

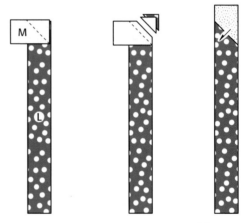

Right Front Leg
Make 1 for each block.

9. Add leg units L/M to opposite sides of dog body J/K and press toward the legs. Sew the head to the upper edge of the body unit. Press toward the head.

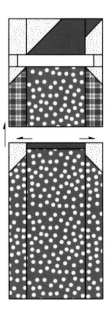

10. Sew background O to one short end of back leg N. Press. Make 1 and 1 reversed.

11. Sew the back-leg units to opposite sides of the dog to complete the block; press. (You will add the hat pompon appliqué later.)

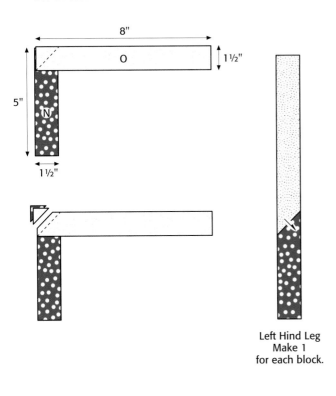

Left Hind Leg
Make 1
for each block.

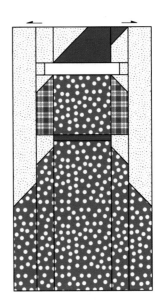

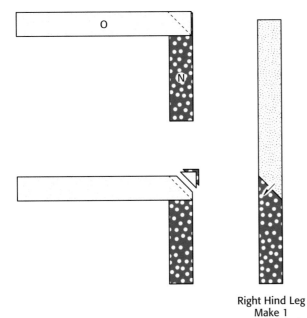

Right Hind Leg
Make 1
for each block.

Making the Sawtooth Star Blocks

Referring to "Flip-and-Sew Piecing" on pages 9–10 and the illustrations below, make 34 Sawtooth Star blocks.

1. Sew star-point squares T to opposite ends of each background U. Make 4 matching units for each star.

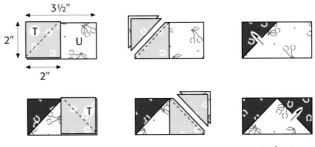

Make 4
for each Star block.

2. Sew background V to opposite ends of 2 of the star-point units for each block.

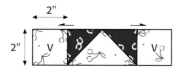

Make 2 for each Star block.

3. Add star-point units T/U to star center W, followed by star-point units T/U/V. Press seams toward the star center.

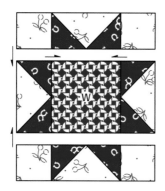

Assembling the Quilt Top

1. Referring to the illustration below, arrange the blocks on a large, flat surface, alternating Santadog blocks (A and B) with *pairs* of Sawtooth Star blocks (C and D) to create a staggered setting. *Do not sew blocks together yet, but keep them in this order as you add the remaining background pieces.*

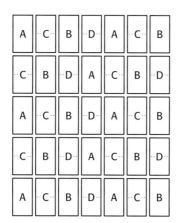

A and B are Santadog blocks.
C and D are pairs of Star blocks.

2. Referring to the diagram, sew a background X to the top edge, and a background Y to the bottom edge of the Santadog blocks in the "A" positions. For the "B" blocks, reverse the position of the X and Y strips. Press the seams toward the background strips.

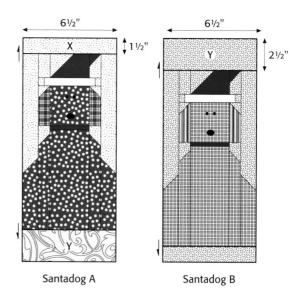

Santadog A   Santadog B

3. Referring to "Adding Appliqués" on pages 11–12 and using template P below, prepare hat pompons; appliqué one to each hat point.

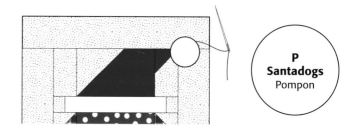

P
Santadogs
Pompon

Dog Talk

Pompons

If you prefer, use fabric yo-yos, large white buttons, large jingle bells, or 1"-diameter fluffy white pompons instead of appliquéd pompons on the hats.

4. Sew a background X to the *bottom* edge of each Sawtooth Star block in the "C" pairs, as shown at right, and then sew the 2 blocks together. Sew a background X to the *top* edge of each Sawtooth Star block in the D pairs, and then sew the 2 blocks together. Press the seam allowances toward the background strips in each unit.

5. Referring to the quilt plan below, sew the blocks together in horizontal rows with 2" x 14½" vertical sashing strips between the blocks. Press the seams toward the sashing strips. Sew the rows together and press the seams toward the background/sashing strips.

6. Referring to "Adding Borders" on page 13, add the inner side borders, followed by the top and bottom borders. Repeat with the outer borders. Press all seams toward the inner borders.

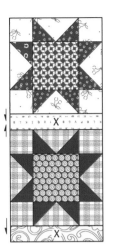

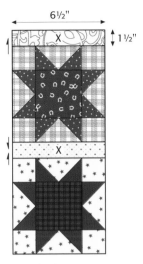

Paired Stars C   Paired Stars D

Quilt Plan

Finishing

Refer to "Finishing the Quilt" on pages 14–16 and "Adding Details" on page 16.

1. Layer the quilt top with batting and backing, and then baste the layers together.
2. Hand or machine quilt as desired. (I used an overall quilting pattern.)
3. Using 2 strands of embroidery floss, satin stitch the dog eyes and noses. If you prefer, cut dot noses from Ultra Suede scraps and stitch in place.
4. Fold bowtie Q in half lengthwise with right sides together. Stitch ¼" from the long raw edges and turn right side out. Finger-press with the seam in the center on the underside of the strip. Fold the short ends to meet in the center over the seam line; hand tack the ends in place with a few stitches. Accordion-pleat the bow 2 or 3 times in the center and take a few hand stitches through the folds to hold them in place. Fasten off stitches.

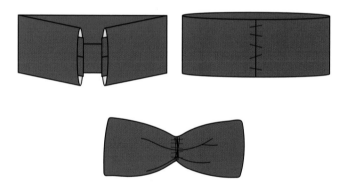

5. Turn under and overlap the long edges of bowtie knot R. Wrap the folded strip around the pleated center of the bow and tack the raw edges together on the back of the bowtie. Sew a bow to the center of each dog collar in the Santadog blocks.

6. Bind the quilt and add a label.

Holiday Place Mats

At 11" tall, the finished Santadog block is just the right size for holiday place mats.

1. For each place mat, cut a 10½" x 11½" piece of background fabric and sew it to one long edge of a Santadog block.
2. Layer the place mat with a 12" x 17" piece of backing and batting.
3. Quilt as desired and bind the outer edges to finish.

Kitty Yo-Yo Wreath

Kids and cat lovers will get a kick out of this quick holiday wreath.
Fabric yo-yos are stiffened with plastic inserts to make them sturdy.

14" diameter, by Janet Kime

Finished Wreath Diameter: 14"

Materials

Yardage is based on 42"-wide fabric, with 40" of usable width after preshrinking.

½ yd. *total* of 12 assorted green fabrics for cats

13" piece of template plastic*

9" metal macramé ring (available at crafts stores)

2 yds. ⅛"-wide red ribbon

Black embroidery floss

White fabric glue

Transparent tape or masking tape

Glue gun and glue

Chalk pencil

In place of template plastic, you can cut the required pieces from the lids of disposable plastic containers. Use sharp scissors to cut the lids.

Making the Kitty Yo-Yos

Use the templates on page 56.

1. From each of the 12 assorted green fabrics, cut 1 template A piece and 1 template B piece. From each fabric, also cut pieces a little smaller than templates C and D. Cut 12 C and 12 D pieces from template plastic.

2. Using white fabric glue, attach the fabric C and D pieces to the plastic pieces, with the right side of the fabric up. Allow the glue to dry.

3. Turn under ¼" on the large fabric circle for the cat body and do a running stitch around the folded edge. Place the fabric-covered circle, fabric side up, in the center on the wrong side of the large fabric circle. Draw up the stitching as snugly as possible, pulling the fabric in around the plastic circle. Secure with several small stitches.

4. Repeat step 3 with the smaller fabric circle and the plastic head form. After drawing up the gathers and fastening off, take a few running stitches up between the 2 ears. Take a few running stitches back toward the center, pulling the thread tightly to draw the fabric down between the ears. Repeat sewing up and back down, pulling the fabric down as far as you can.

5. On the side with the gathered opening, fold the excess fabric between the ears to one side and tack down. Repeat on the other side.

6. Embroider the eyes on the side without gathers, using 2 strands of embroidery floss to make small French knots.

7. With the head overlapping the top edge on the gathered side of the body circle, sew the head in place with a few hand stitches.

8. For each cat, tie a bow in a 6"-long piece of ribbon and glue in place at the bottom of the head.

Assembling the Wreath

1. Referring to the photo on page 53, arrange the 12 cats in a circle, face down, overlapping the bodies slightly at their widest points. Place the macramé ring on the circle and adjust the positions of the cats as necessary so the ring lies at the widest point of each cat.

2. Temporarily attach each cat to the ring with a piece of transparent or masking tape.

3. Using a glue gun, glue the macramé ring to the cat backs. Remove the tape from one cat at a time and mark with a chalk pencil where the ring will lie. Glue, wait for the glue to set, and then glue the next cat until all are securely attached.

Kitty Yo-Yo Ornament

Make single yo-yo kitties for Christmas ornaments or package ties. Add a loop of clear nylon thread for hanging.

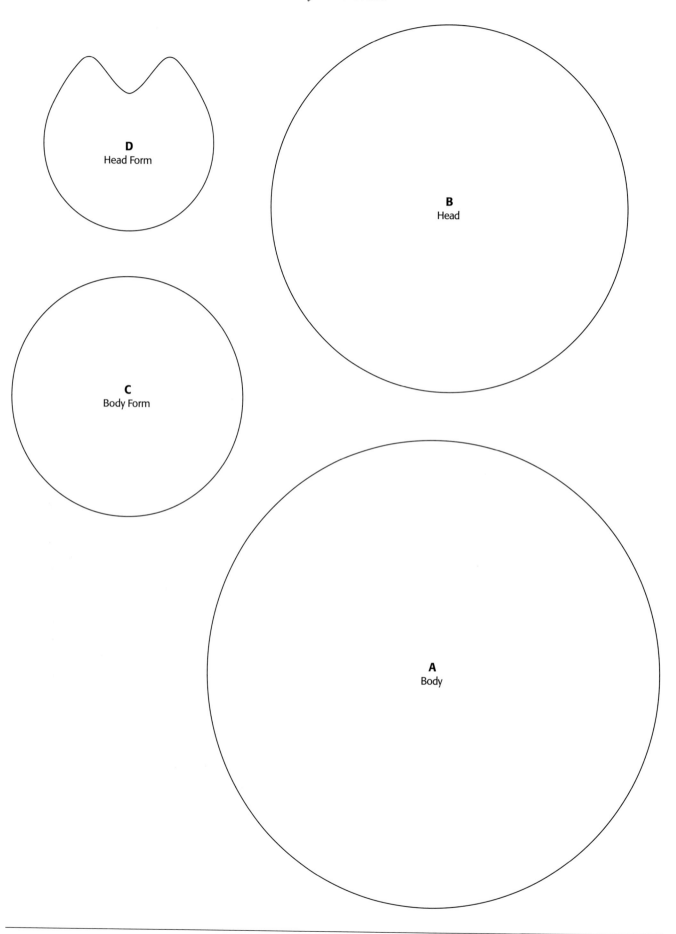

My Dog's an Angel

Robert B. Parker wrote in Potshot, *"I heard somebody define heaven once as a place where, when you get there, all the dogs you ever loved run to greet you." Immortalize your own little angel with this heartfelt Christmas wall hanging.*

26" x 26", by Karen Gabriel

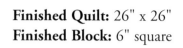

Finished Quilt: 26" x 26"
Finished Block: 6" square

Angeldog Block

Heart Block

Materials

Yardage is based on 42"-wide fabric, with 40" of usable width after preshrinking.

Assorted fabric scraps for angels, hearts, and outer pieced border

¼ yd. 45"-wide silver lamé for wings and middle border

1 yd. for block background, inner border, and binding

1 yd. for backing

28" x 28" piece of batting

1 yd. ⅛"-diameter silver cord

Black embroidery floss

Optional: Ultra Suede for nose appliqués

Cutting

Refer to "Making the Blocks" below for appliqué directions. Refer to "Piecing the Outer Borders" on page 59 for outer-border cutting directions. *Cut all strips across the fabric width (crosswise grain).*

Background and Inner Border

Piece	No. of Pieces	Dimensions
Binding	3	2¾" x 40"
Side inner borders	2	1½" x 18½"
Top and bottom inner borders	2	1½" x 20½"
Appliqué background	9	7" x 7"

Middle Border

Piece	No. of Pieces	Dimensions
Side borders	2	1" x 20½"
Top and bottom borders	2	1" x 21½"

Making the Blocks

Use the templates on page 61.

1. Referring to "Adding Appliqués" on pages 11–12, cut and prepare hearts A, wings B, dog bodies C, and ears D. To reduce bulk, do not turn under the long straight edge on each wing. Press the prepared shapes.

2. Position and sew the appliqués to the background squares, making 5 Angeldog blocks and 4 Heart blocks. Use the crosses on the pattern pieces for centering the pieces on the blocks.

On the dog blocks, appliqué the wings B first, followed by the dog body C, which should cover the unturned straight edges of the wings. Appliqué ears D last, tucking the ends of a 7"-long piece of silver cord under the ears for the halo. Hand tack the halo in place. Tilt the halos in different directions.

3. Embroider the dogs' eyes (French knots) and mouths (satin stitch), reversing the tilt of the mouth on some of them. Satin stitch the dogs' noses, or cut them from Ultra Suede scraps and appliqué by hand.

4. Press the completed blocks and trim each block to 6½" x 6½".

Assembling the Quilt Top

1. Referring to the photo, arrange the blocks in 3 horizontal rows of 3 blocks each and sew together in rows. Press the seams in opposite directions from row to row.

2. Sew the rows together and press the seams in one direction.

3. Referring to "Adding Borders" on page 13, sew the side inner borders to the quilt top, followed by the top and bottom inner borders.

4. Repeat with the silver lamé middle borders. Press the seams toward the inner border strips, taking care with the iron to avoid damaging the lamé.

Dog Talk

Working with Metallic Fabrics

Be careful when pressing metallic fabrics; many melt easily, even with your iron set at a low temperature. Experiment with a scrap of the fabric first. If you can't get a good press at a low iron setting, turn the seam allowances to one side and run your thumbnail down the right side of the seam along the stitching line to press.

Piecing the Outer Borders

1. From the assorted fabrics, cut 3½"-long strips in varying widths from 1½" to 3".

2. From one fabric, cut 4 matching corner squares, 3½" x 3½".

3. Sew the long edges of the 3½"-long strips together in random order to make 4 outer border strips, 3½" x 21½".

4. Sew a corner square to the opposite ends of 2 of the pieced outer border strips to complete the top and bottom border strips.

5. Sew the side outer border strips to the quilt and press the seams toward the middle border. Add the top and bottom outer border strips and press.

Quilt Plan

Finishing

Refer to "Finishing the Quilt" on pages 14–16.

1. Layer the quilt top with batting and backing, and then baste the layers together.

2. Hand or machine quilt around each dog and heart. Quilt the borders as desired.

3. Bind the quilt and add a label.

Angeldog Ornament

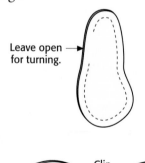

To make an Angeldog ornament, you'll need fabric scraps and templates A, C, and D. (Use the heart template for the wings instead of the wing template used in the quilt.) You will also need a small piece of template plastic for the wings, a 2½"-diameter gold macramé ring for the halo, a handful of polyester fiberfill, and clear nylon thread for a hanging loop.

1. Place fabric right sides together for each piece and trace around each template on the appropriate fabric.

2. For the wings and ears, stitch on the drawn lines, leaving a 1"-long opening for turning the ears and at least a 3"-long opening for the wings. Cut out the pieces ¼" from the wing stitching and ⅛" from the ear stitching. Clip the curves and the inside corner of the wings.

3. Turn the ears and wing piece right side out. On the ears, turn under the open edges and slipstitch closed. For the wings, cut a piece of flexible template plastic ⅛" *smaller all around* than the heart template A and insert into the wing piece. Slipstitch the opening closed.

4. Cut out 2 dog bodies from matching fabric, adding a ¼"-wide seam allowance all around. Embroider the dog's face on the right side of one of the 2 body pieces.

5. Sew the bodies with right sides together, stitching on the drawn line and leaving a 2"-long opening at one upper side edge. Turn the body right side out, stuff with fiberfill, and slipstitch the opening closed.

6. Sew a 2½"-diameter macramé ring to the back of the dog's head for a halo. Tack the wings in place on the back of the dog.

7. Use clear nylon thread to make a hanging loop.

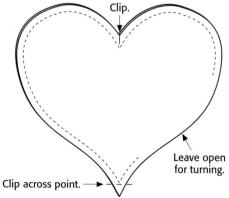

Leave open for turning.

Clip.

Leave open for turning.

Clip across point.

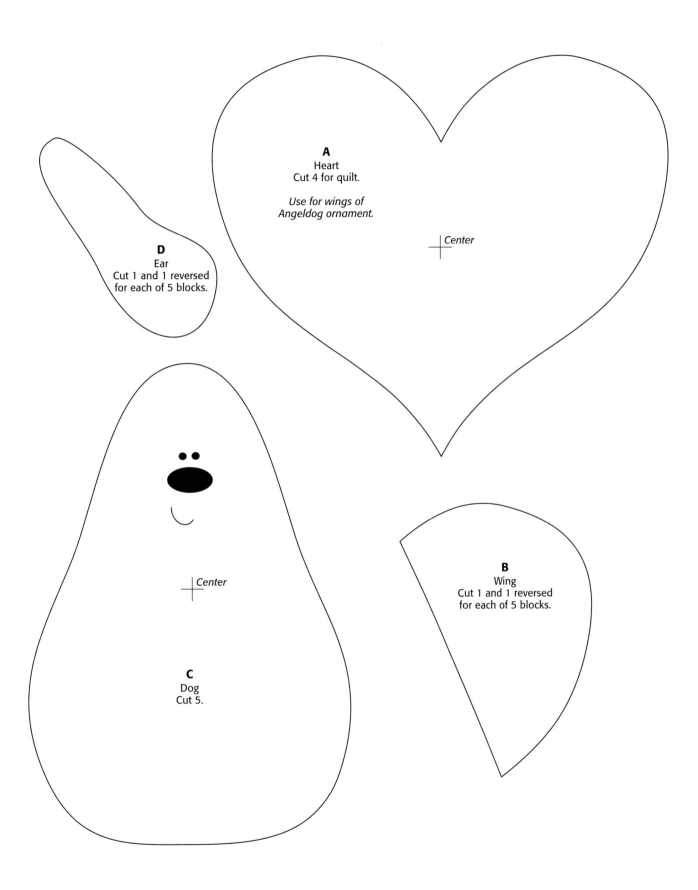

A
Heart
Cut 4 for quilt.

*Use for wings of
Angeldog ornament.*

⊢ *Center*

D
Ear
Cut 1 and 1 reversed
for each of 5 blocks.

B
Wing
Cut 1 and 1 reversed
for each of 5 blocks.

⊢ *Center*

C
Dog
Cut 5.

Kitten Garland

*Kittens in holiday dresses are tied together with bright ribbon bows to make a garland
for your tree, window, or fireplace mantel. Without the ribbons, they make
individual Christmas ornaments for all your cat-loving friends.*

by Janet Kime

Finished Kitten: 3¾" tall

Materials

Assorted fabric scraps for kittens and dresses

20"-long piece of ¼"-wide ribbon for each kitten

Template plastic

Polyester fiberfill stuffing

Black seed beads for eyes

White fabric glue

Making the Kittens

Use the template on page 64 to make as many kittens as desired.

1. Trace the kitten pattern onto template plastic and cut out.

2. For each kitten, place 2 matching pieces of kitten fabric right sides together. On the wrong side of 1 piece, draw around the kitten template.

3. Cut a 1"-long vertical slit in the center back of *1 piece only.*

4. For each kitten, cut 2 pieces of ribbon, each 10" long. Slip one end of each piece through the vertical slit and out the end of a front paw as shown. The ribbon should extend about ¼" beyond the drawn line at the end of the paw. Pin in place.

5. Stitch on the drawn line around each kitten, catching the ribbon in the stitching at the ends of the front paws. Stitch over the beginning of the stitching for ½" to secure. Trim excess fabric, leaving a ⅛"-wide seam allowance all around. Clip the inside curves and between the legs to within a thread or two of the stitching.

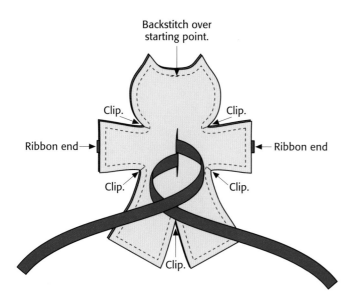

6. Turn the kitten right side out through the slit and stuff lightly with fiberfill. Whipstitch the slit closed. Sew on seed beads for eyes.

Cat Chat

Turning Points

To turn smooth corners and points, use a wooden point turner (from the notions department) or use a thick pin or a large, sharp needle to pull out the corners of the paws and the ear tips.

7. For each dress, cut a 4" x 6" piece of fabric. Turn under and press ¼" on both long edges.

8. Fold in half with right sides together and raw unpressed edges even. Stitch ¼" from the short raw edges as shown. Finger-press the seam open, and then re-press the upper and lower folded edges and turn right side out.

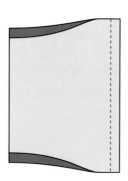

9. With wrong sides together, fold the resulting fabric tube so that the folded edges are even. The lower folded edge is the bottom of the dress. (See illustration on page 64.)

10. Adjust so the seam is in the center back and cut ½"-long slits for armholes as shown, starting the slits ¼" below the upper edge of the dress.

    Thread a sewing needle with a 20"-long piece of thread and double it but don't knot the end. Beginning at the center back and leaving a 4"-long thread tail, do a running stitch around the dress ⅛" from the upper edge of the dress, stitching through all the layers. Cut the thread, leaving another 4"-long thread tail.

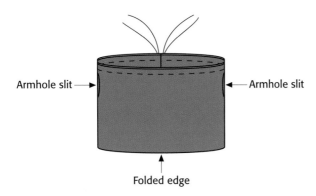

Armhole slit ←   → Armhole slit

Folded edge

11. Pull the dress over the kitten's head, pulling the front legs through the slits in the dress. Using the thread tails, pull up the running stitches to gather the neck of the dress. Knot the threads together at the back to hold the gathers in place but don't trim the thread ends yet.

12. With a pin or needle, tuck under the raw edges around each armhole and any frayed threads. Hold in place with a few dabs of white glue between the dress fabric and the kitten front leg.

Cat Chat

Gluing in Small Spaces

If the nozzle on your glue bottle is too big to fit between the dress and the kitten, pour a small amount of glue onto a piece of scrap paper and use a toothpick to pick up just a drop.

13. Trim the thread ends on the back of the dress and secure the knot with a dot of white glue. Set the kitten aside until the glue is dry.

Assembling the Garland

1. Arrange the kittens, spacing them 8" apart.
2. Tie the ribbons together with bows. It's easier to do this if you hold the kitten on each side firmly in place. A helper could do this for you. If you're working alone, use pins to hold the kittens firmly on a thick piece of corrugated cardboard or a piece of Styrofoam packing material.

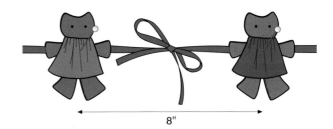

8"

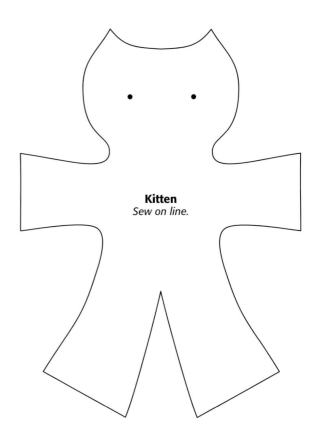

Kitten
Sew on line.

Maurice at Christmas

Black-and-white tuxedo cats are always attired for a formal affair and
they look great in Christmas-colored accessories. Choose a wonderful
Christmas print for the border of this simple appliqué project.

22" x 30", by Virginia Morrison

Materials

Yardage is based on 42"-wide fabric, with 40" of usable width after preshrinking.

¼ yd. black for cat bodies and faces

Assorted black, white, red, green, and brown fabric scraps for cat faces, hat, muffler, tree, tree trunk, and star

½ yd. light-colored fabric for background

1 yd. bold Christmas print for border and binding

¾ yd. for backing

32" x 24" piece of batting

4 buttons, ½" diameter, for eyes

Black embroidery floss

Optional: Ultra Suede for nose appliqués

Cutting

Refer to "Appliquéing the Cats" at right for cutting the appropriate appliqué pieces.

Background

Piece	No. of Pieces	Dimensions
	1	23½" x 15½"

Border and Binding

Piece	No. of Pieces	Dimensions
Top and bottom borders	2	4½" x 22½"
Side borders	2	4½" x 22½"
Binding	3	2¾" x 40"

Appliquéing the Cats

Use the templates on pages 68–69.

1. Referring to "Adding Appliqués" on pages 11–12, cut and prepare each appliqué piece using the paper-patch method. For each cat, cut 1 and 1 reversed of cat face C (4 total).

   To reduce bulk, don't turn under the top edge of cat body A, the bottom edge of hat D, the ends of muffler G and H that will tuck under muffler I, and the top edge of tree trunk J. Turn under only the bottom edge of cat nose B.

2. Locate and mark the center point of the background piece as described on page 12. Center the tree piece L and arrange the remaining pieces in alphabetical order from J to Q. Appliqué in alphabetical order so each piece overlaps the previous one. Appliqué star R above the tree.

3. Position the cat appliqués on each side of the tree, leaving about ¾" between tree piece K and the cat bodies. *Make sure that there is at least 1" of background fabric beyond the outer edges of the appliqué pieces.*

4. Sew cat body A in place first, then nose B, and finally face C. For the left-hand cat, appliqué hat D, then brim E, and pompon F. For the right-hand cat, appliqué muffler G and H, then cover the raw edges with muffler I.

Cat Chat

Appliquéing Pinned Pieces

It can be difficult to appliqué when you have several pieces pinned in place; your thread will loop around the pins as you sew. Here's a simple way to prevent this problem.

1. Pin the pieces in place on the front of the appliqué panel.
2. Flip the panel over and re-pin the appliqués from the back. To avoid stabbing your fingers, tuck the sharp ends of the pins back into the background fabric, but not all the way through the appliqués on the front.
3. Remove the pins on the front and stitch the appliqués in place.

Pin appliqués in place on right side.

Re-pin on wrong side.

Remove pins on right side before stitching.

5. Embroider the cats' noses with a satin stitch, or cut them from Ultra Suede and appliqué them by hand.
6. Press the completed appliqué panel and trim to 14½" x 22½".
7. Referring to "Adding Borders" on page 13, sew the top and bottom borders to the appliqué panel, followed by the side borders. Press all seams toward the borders.

Finishing

Refer to "Finishing the Quilt" on pages 14–16.
1. Layer the quilt top with batting and backing, and then baste the layers together.
2. Quilt around each cat and around the outer edges of the tree. Quilt in-the-ditch along the seam line between the background and the border. Do additional quilting in the border if desired.
3. Sew on the button eyes.
4. Bind the quilt and add a label.

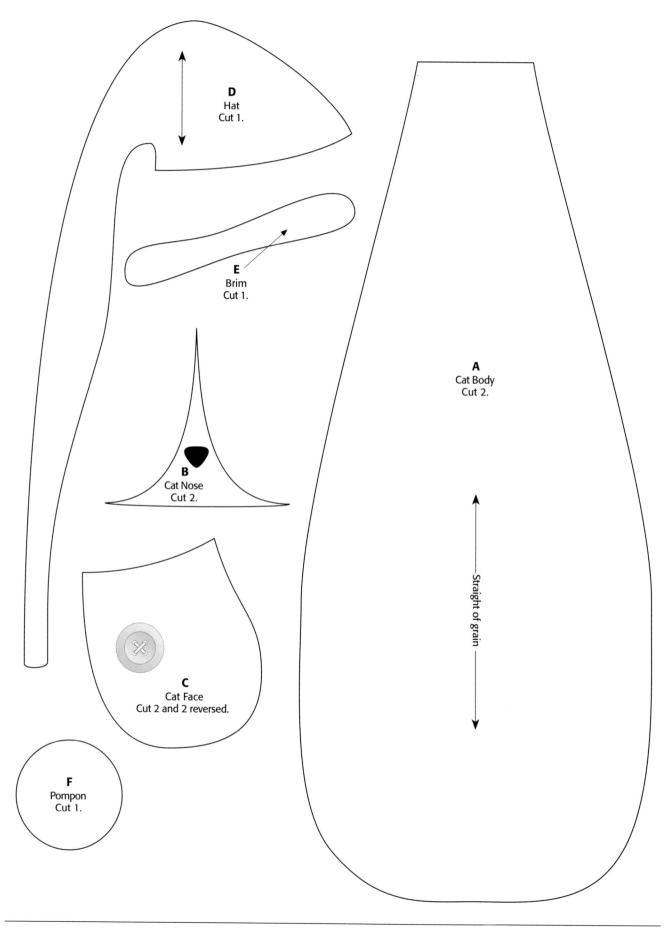

D
Hat
Cut 1.

E
Brim
Cut 1.

A
Cat Body
Cut 2.

Straight of grain

B
Cat Nose
Cut 2.

C
Cat Face
Cut 2 and 2 reversed.

F
Pompon
Cut 1.

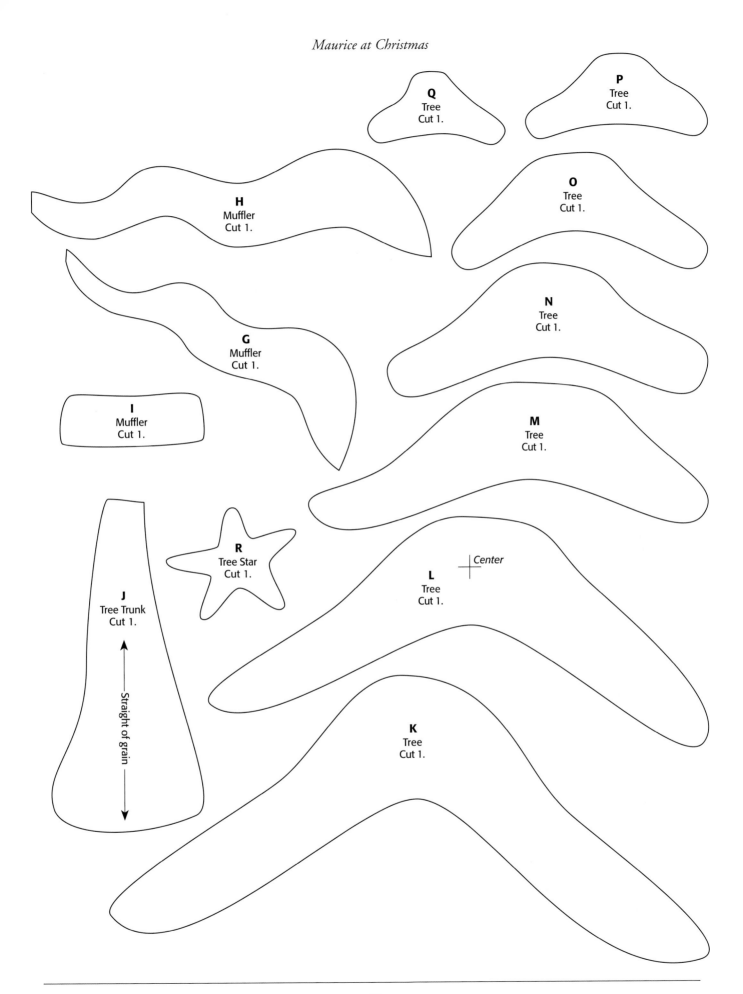

Q
Tree
Cut 1.

P
Tree
Cut 1.

H
Muffler
Cut 1.

O
Tree
Cut 1.

G
Muffler
Cut 1.

N
Tree
Cut 1.

I
Muffler
Cut 1.

M
Tree
Cut 1.

R
Tree Star
Cut 1.

Center

L
Tree
Cut 1.

J
Tree Trunk
Cut 1.

Straight of grain

K
Tree
Cut 1.

"Amewsing" Grace

This demure little angel in a hoop is a quick appliqué project for door or wall decoration.
You could also make several as blocks and sew them together to make a small quilt.

9" diameter, by Virginia Morrison

Materials

Yardage is based on 42"-wide fabric, with 40" of usable width after preshrinking.

Assorted fabric scraps for cat, dress, and wings

½ yd. for background and backing

13" square of batting

Black embroidery floss

12"-long piece of perle cotton for neck bow

7 buttons, ¼" diameter, for halo

White fabric glue

9"-diameter wooden quilting or embroidery hoop

Making the Angel

Use the templates on page 73.

1. From each of 2 dress fabrics, cut a strip 1" x 6". With strips right sides together, stitch ¼" from the long edges. Press the seam toward the darker fabric in the strip unit. Cut 5 segments, 1" wide, from the strip unit.

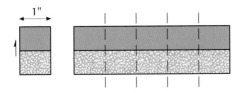

2. Sew the segments together as shown to make a checkerboard band.

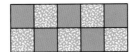

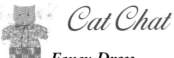

Cat Chat

Fancy Dress

Instead of fabric scraps, you can use a lace-edged or embroidered handkerchief for the angel's dress. Prepare it as usual, using the paper-patch appliqué technique described on pages 11–12, but arrange it so the finished or lace edge of the handkerchief lies along the bottom edge of the dress and leave that edge open for a little added dimension. If the handkerchief is sheer, line it with a hemmed piece of matching cotton fabric, before you prepare it for appliqué.

3. Cut 2 pieces of dress fabric, one 2½" x 3" and one ¾" x 3". Sew one to each long edge of the checkerboard band. Press the seams toward the dress fabrics.

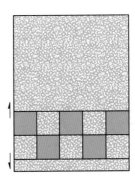

4. Trace the templates on page 73 onto heavy paper and cut out on the drawn lines. Pin the paper patch for dress B to the wrong side of the dress, with the lower edge of the paper ¼" above the bottom edge. Trim away excess fabric, leaving a ¼"-wide allowance all around. Turn the allowance over the paper edge and baste as described for paper-pieced appliqué on pages 11–12. *Do not turn under the top edge of the dress.*

5. Using the desired fabrics, prepare 2 wings A in the same manner, making 1 reversed. Prepare 2 sleeves D, making 1 reversed. Prepare 1 head E and 2 paws C. *Do not turn under the straight edges of the paws.* Press all prepared appliqués.

6. Cut a 13" square of background fabric. Find and mark the center of the square as described on page 12. Using the placement diagram on page 73 as a guide, place the small cross on the center of the background fabric. Sew wings A to the background fabric, followed by the dress, paws, and sleeves in that order. Add the head last.

7. Use 2 strands of black embroidery floss to satin stitch the cat's eyes.

Finishing

1. Layer the completed appliqué panel with the batting and backing fabric and baste.

2. Quilt around the angel and sew buttons in an arc above the head to make the halo.

3. Place the *inner* hoop of the 9" hoop on the remaining backing fabric. Using the outside of the hoop as a guide, draw a circle on the fabric. Cut out the circle on the drawn line. Turn under and baste ¼" around the outer edge of the circle. Press, remove the basting, and set aside the circle for step 5.

4. Center the quilted piece over the inner hoop; add the outer hoop and tighten, making sure the tightening screw is centered at the top of the design. On the underside, trim away the excess

fabric and batting, leaving a ½"-wide allowance all around. Remove the basting threads.

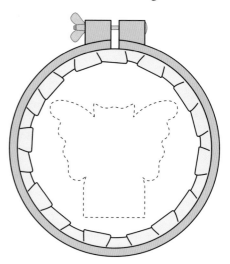

5. With the fabric right side facing you, pin the backing circle in place over the back of the hoop to cover the raw edges. Begin by placing a pin at opposite sides of the circle at 12 o'clock and 6 o'clock; add 2 more pins on opposite sides at 3 o'clock and 9 o'clock. Pin the remainder in place and slipstitch the circle to the quilted panel. Remove the pins.

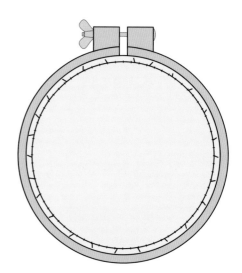

Slipstitch circle in place.

6. Tie a bow in the strand of perle cotton and tack it to the neck of the dress. Tack the loops and ends of the bow in place with a few drops of white glue.

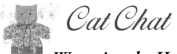

Cat Chat

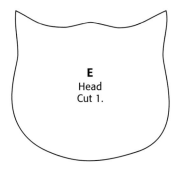

Wrapping the Hoop with Ribbon

You can wrap the outer hoop with ribbon for a more festive decoration.

1. Loosen the outer hoop *only after you have sewn the backing circle in place.*

2. Wrap a pretty ribbon around and around the outer hoop only and secure the ends with a dot of glue.

3. Retighten the outer hoop and add a pretty ribbon bow to camouflage the tightening screw.

Placement Diagram

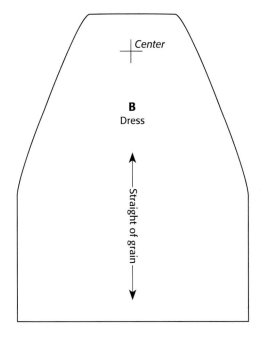

E
Head
Cut 1.

Center

B
Dress

Straight of grain

A
Wing
Cut 1 and 1 reversed.

C
Paw
Cut 2.

D
Sleeve
Cut 1 and
1 reversed.

Night "Mewsic"

Sparkling Ohio Stars alternate with colorful cats, each sporting a jaunty bowtie with a button for a knot. The stars reminded the quilt's maker of Mozart's "Eine Kleine Nachtmusik" (A Little Night Music), hence the quilt's name.

62" x 73", by Virginia Morrison; quilted by Nancy Weed

Finished Quilt: 62" x 73"
Finished Bowtie Cat Block: 6" x 11"
Finished Ohio Star Block: 6" x 6"

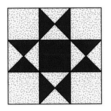

Bowtie Cat Block   Ohio Star Block

Materials

Yardage is based on 42"-wide fabric, with 40" of usable width after preshrinking.

1 yd. *total* of assorted prints for cat legs, outer faces, and ears

½ yd. assorted prints for cat tummies and inner faces

½ yd. assorted prints for Ohio Star blocks

Assorted scraps for bowties

3 yds. light print for block backgrounds, sashing strips, and inner border

2 yds. for outer border and binding

4 yds. for backing

64" x 75" piece of batting

18 buttons for bowties, ½" to ¾" diameter

Embroidery floss

Cutting

To keep them in order, put all the pieces for each cat and each star in its own self-sealing plastic bag. Cut 18 cats, each from a combination of 3 fabrics—1 for the body, 1 for the tummy and face, and 1 for the bowtie.

Cat Legs, Outer Face, and Ears

Piece	No. of Pieces	Dimensions
A (back leg)	2	1½" x 5½"
B (front leg)	2	1½" x 7½"
C (face)	2	1½" x 3½"
D (face)	1	2½" x 1¼"
E (face)	2	1" x 1"
F (ear)	2	1½" x 1½"

Cat Tummy and Inner Face

Piece	No. of Pieces	Dimensions
G (tummy)	1	2½" x 7½"
H (face)	1	2½" x 2¾"

Bowtie

Piece	No. of Pieces	Dimensions
I	4	1½" x 1½"

Ohio Star Blocks

Cut pieces for 17 stars, each star from a different fabric.

Piece	No. of Pieces	Dimensions
M (center)	1	2½" x 2½"
N (points)	2	3¼" x 3¼"

Sashing, Inner Borders, and Background

Cut the sashing and inner border strips parallel to the selvages, and then cut the other pieces from the remaining fabric.

Piece	No. of Pieces	Dimensions
Vertical sashing	30	1½" x 11½"
Horizontal sashing	4	1½" x 48½"
Side borders	2	1½" x 59½"
Top and bottom borders	2	1½" x 50½"

Cat Background

Piece	No. of Pieces	Dimensions
J	36	1½" x 7½"
K	72	1½" x 1½"
L	18	1½" x 4½"

Ohio Star Background

Piece	No. of Pieces	Dimensions
O	68	2½" x 2½"
P	34	3¼" x 3¼"
Q	17	4½" x 6½"
R	17	1½" x 6½"

Outer Border and Binding

Cut all strips parallel to the selvages.

Piece	No. of Pieces	Dimensions
Side borders	2	6½" x 61½"
Top and bottom borders	2	6½" x 62½"
Binding	4	2¾" x 72"

Making the Bowtie Cat Blocks

Referring to "Flip-and-Sew Piecing" on pages 9–10 and the illustrations below, make 18 Bowtie Cat blocks.

To make each block:
1. Sew a back leg A to a background J. Repeat, making a mirror image of the first A/J unit. Press as directed. Set aside.

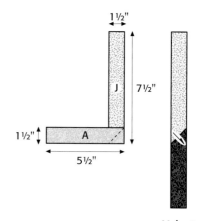

Make 1
for each block.

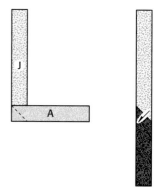

Make 1
for each block.

2. Sew a background K to a front leg B. Repeat, making a mirror image of the first B/K unit. Press as directed.

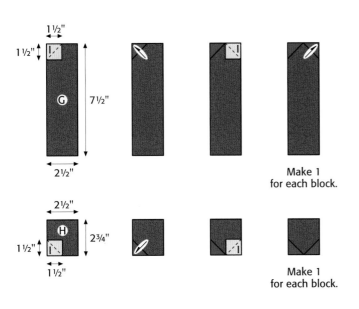

Make 1
for each block.

Make 1
for each block.

3. Sew a bowtie I to each upper corner of tummy G and press toward the bowtie. Repeat with the lower corners of head H.

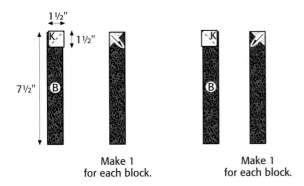

Make 1
for each block.

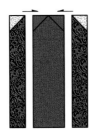

Make 1
for each block.

4. Sew a front-leg unit to opposite long edges of the tummy unit. Set aside.

5. Sew a head E to each upper corner of the face unit from step 3 and press as directed.

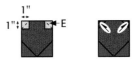

6. Sew a head D to the upper edge of the face unit and press as directed.

7. Sew a background K to a face C. Repeat to make a mirror image of the first C/K unit. Press as directed.

Make 1
for each block.

Make 1
for each block.

8. Sew a C/K head unit to each side of the face unit and press as directed.

9. Sew an ear F to opposite ends of background L and press. Sew to the top edge of the head unit.

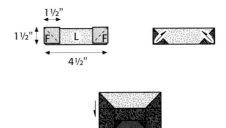

10. Sew the head unit to the cat body unit from step 4. *Press the seam allowances open* to distribute the bulk.

11. Sew the back-leg A/J units from step 1 to opposite sides of the cat body unit to complete the block. Press toward the back legs.

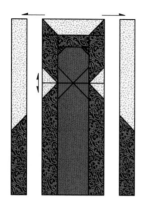

Press seam open
between head and body.

12. Embroider the cats' eyes, using 2 strands of black embroidery thread and doing a satin stitch.

Making the Ohio Star Blocks

Referring to "Making Half-Square-Triangle Units" on page 10 and the following illustrations, make 17 Ohio Star blocks.

For each block:

1. Draw a diagonal line on the wrong side of each of the 3¼" background squares.

2. With right sides together, stitch each 3¼" background square to a 3¼" star square, stitching a scant ¼" from the line on each side. Press to set the stitches, and then cut on the drawn line.

Press the seam toward the star fabric in each half-square-triangle unit.

3. Draw a diagonal line on the wrong side of each triangle unit, perpendicular to the seam line. With right sides together (make sure contrasting colors are opposite each other) and the seams nesting into each other, sew 2 matching half-square-triangle units together. Stitch a scant ¼" on both sides of the drawn line. Press. Cut on the line and press the seam in one direction in each resulting pieced square.

Make 4 for each block.

4. Repeat with the same star fabric to make 2 more pieced squares for a total of 4 for each block.

5. Arrange the pieced squares with a matching center square M and 4 background squares O. Sew together in horizontal rows and press the seams in the direction of the arrows.

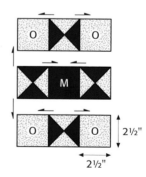

6. Sew background R to the top edge and background Q to the bottom edge of each Ohio Star block. Press seams toward the background pieces.

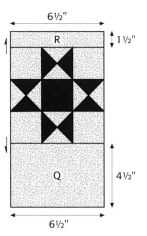

Assembling the Quilt Top

1. Referring to the illustration below, arrange the Bowtie Cat and Ohio Star blocks in horizontal rows with 11½"-long background sashing strips between them. Note that the star blocks are rotated so that some have a wide background strip at the top and others have a narrow strip at the top. This creates a staggered setting for more visual interest.
2. Sew the blocks and sashing strips together in horizontal rows and press all seams toward the sashing strips.
3. Sew the horizontal rows together, with a horizontal sashing strip between each pair of rows. Press seams toward the sashing strips.

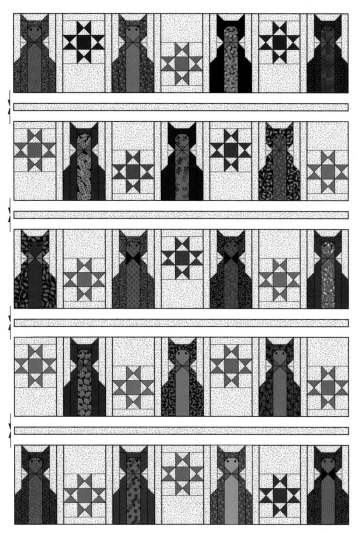

Quilt Assembly

4. Referring to "Adding Borders" on page 13, sew the inner side borders to the long edges of the quilt top, followed by the top and bottom inner borders. Press all seams toward the border strips. Repeat with the outer borders.

Finishing

Refer to "Finishing the Quilt" on pages 14–16.

1. Layer the quilt top with batting and backing, and then baste the layers together.
2. Machine quilt as desired. The sample quilt was quilted in an overall design.
3. Sew a button to the center of each bowtie.
4. Bind the quilt and add a label.

 Cat Chat

Self-Covered Buttons

If you can't find buttons to match your bowtie fabrics, cover the buttons with fabric to match each tie.

1. Cut a fabric circle twice the diameter of the button and do a running stitch ⅛" from the outer edge.
2. Place the button on the wrong side of the circle and pull up the gathers with the button inside. Fasten the gathering thread by taking a few backstitches.
3. From the back of the button, poke the point of a large needle through each of the button's holes, so you can see where they are on the front of the fabric-covered button.
4. Sew on the button as usual.

Cattycanes

These slender cats are all decked out for the holidays with their candy-cane tails.

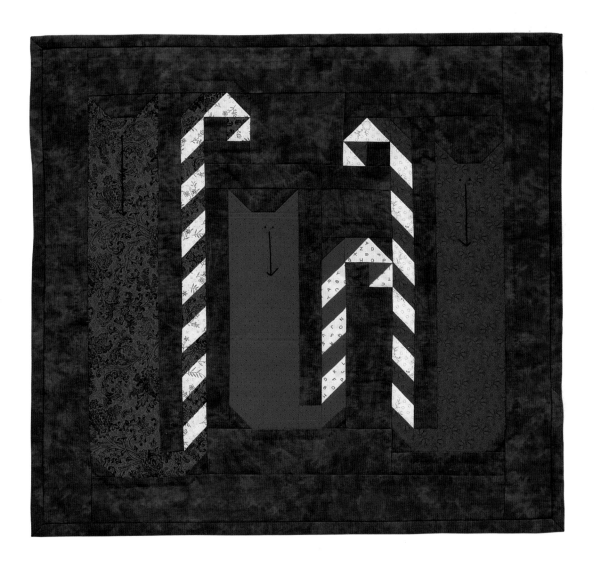

20" x 22", by Janet Kime

Materials

Yardage is based on 42"-wide fabric, with 40" of usable width after preshrinking.

¼ yd. *each* or 1 fat quarter of 3 different fabrics for cats

Scraps of 3 different light prints for candy cane stripes

⅔ yd. for block background, border, and binding

¾ yd. for backing

21" x 23" piece of batting

Black embroidery floss

Cutting

Note: *Keep the pieces organized in 3 small, self-sealing plastic bags labeled with the cat number.*

Cat Fabrics

Cat 1

Piece	No. of Pieces	Dimensions
A (body)	1	3½" x 15½"
B (ears/tail)	4	1½" x 1½"
C (tail stripe)	7	1¼" x 3"
D (tail)	1	1⅞" x 1⅞", *cut in half diagonally (discard 1 triangle)*

Cat 2

Piece	No. of Pieces	Dimensions
E (body)	1	3½" x 9½"
B (ears/tail)	4	1½" x 1½"
C (tail stripe)	3	1¼" x 3"
D (tail)	1	1⅞" x 1⅞", *cut in half diagonally (discard 1 triangle)*

Cat 3

Piece	No. of Pieces	Dimensions
F (body)	1	3½" x 12½"
B (ears/tail)	4	1½" x 1½"
C (tail stripe)	6	1¼" x 3"
D (tail)	1	1⅞" x 1⅞", *cut in half diagonally (discard 1 triangle)*

Light Prints

Cat 1

Piece	No. of Pieces	Dimensions
V	7	1¼" x 3"
W	1	1½" x 2½"
X	1	1⅞" x 1⅞", *cut in half diagonally (discard one triangle)*

Cat 2

Piece	No. of Pieces	Dimensions
V	3	1¼" x 3"
W	1	1½" x 2½"
X	1	1⅞" x 1⅞", *cut in half diagonally (discard one triangle)*

Cat 3

Piece	No. of Pieces	Dimensions
V	6	1¼" x 3"
W	1	1½" x 2½"
X	1	1⅞" x 1⅞", *cut in half diagonally (discard one triangle)*

Background and Borders

Piece	No. of Pieces	Dimensions
G	2	1½" x 3½"
H	15	1½" x 1½"
I	1	1½" x 15½"
J	2	1½" x 2½"
K	1	1½" x 10½"
L	1	1½" x 9½"
M	1	2½" x 6½"
N	2	2½" x 3½"
O	1	1½" x 8½"
P	1	2½" x 8½"
Q	1	1½" x 13½"
R	2	1½" x 5½"
S	1	3½" x 4½"
T (border)	2	2½" x 18½"
U (border)	2	2½" x 20½"

Binding

Piece	No. of Pieces	Dimensions
	3	2¾" x 40"

Making Cat 1

Referring to "Flip-and-Sew Piecing" on pages 9–10 and the illustrations below, make Cat 1.

Use the templates on page 89.

1. Sew 2 ears B to background G.

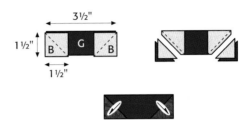

2. Sew the ear unit B/G to the top edge of cat body A. Sew a background H to the lower left corner of the B/G/A unit. Sew a square B (tail) to the lower end of background I. Sew the resulting strip to the right edge of the cat body unit A/B/G/H and press the seam toward the background strip.

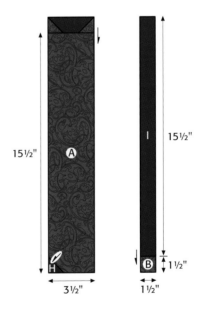

3. To foundation-piece the long tail section, trace the templates on page 89; cut them out and tape together, end to end, carefully matching the arrows.

4. Cut a 1½" x 2⅞" piece of cat fabric 1. Using the grid on your rotary cutting mat and the 45°-angle line on your rotary ruler, trim a triangle from one end of the piece as shown. Discard the triangle.

5. Pin the remainder of the trimmed strip to the lower end of the tail pattern, right side up and edges matching. The angled edge should lie along the first dotted line.

6. Place a light print V on the tail pattern, right side down with the long edge on the first dotted line, as shown. The lower end, where you start stitching, should extend a generous ¼" beyond the dotted line. Stitch a generous ¼" from the dotted line, stitching through the paper pattern. Flip V right side up, over the seam, and press

with a dry iron. The raw edge of V should lie just short of the next dotted line. If it covers the dotted line, trim the piece so the line just shows. Try taking a more generous seam allowance with the next seam.

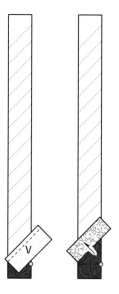

7. Place a cat-fabric C piece on the tail pattern, right side down with the long edge on the dotted line. Stitch ¼" from the dotted line. Flip C right side up, over the seam, and press with a dry iron.

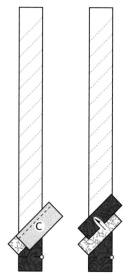

8. Repeat steps 6 and 7, ending with piece C. With the paper side up, trim away excess fabric, cutting along the edges of the paper pattern. The finished piece should measure 1½" x 16½". Sew a background H to the lower end of the tail as shown. Repeat with another H at the top of the tail, lining up the edges of H with the edges of the paper pattern. Tear away the paper, taking care not to pull the stitches out.

9. Sew the striped tail strip to the cat unit from step 2 and press the seam toward the background strip.

10. Sew a cat square B to the left end of piece W. Add a background H to the opposite end.

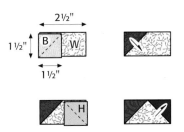

11. Sew tail triangle D to tail triangle X along the long edges. Press toward D. Add a background H to the left edge as shown. Press toward H.

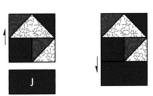

12. Sew the units from steps 10 and 11 together as shown and add a piece J to the lower edge. Press in the direction of the arrows. Set Cat 1 pieces aside while you make Cats 2 and 3.

Cat Chat

Stitching on Paper

When you sew the striped tails, use a smaller than normal stitch length; the more holes you make in the paper pattern, the more easily it will tear away. It also helps to crease the paper on the stitching line just before tearing it.

Making Cat 2

1. Repeat steps 1 and 2 for Cat 1, using the fabric pieces for Cat 2 and background L in place of piece I.

2. Using the tail pattern for Cat 2 on page 89, piece the tail as directed for Cat 1 in steps 3–8. You will need 3 each of light print V and cat piece C. After trimming, the piece should measure 1½" x 8½".

3. Piece the remainder of the tail as directed for Cat 1 in steps 10–12. Add background M to the lower edge of the tail unit. Press. Add the striped tail unit to the left edge of the resulting unit. Press the seam toward background M.

4. Add background N to the upper edge of the tail unit and press the seam toward the background piece.

5. Sew the completed tail unit to the cat body and press as directed.

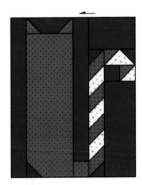

6. Add background K, followed by background O and P. Press all seams toward the background pieces.

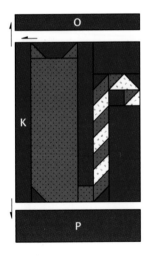

Making Cat 3

1. Repeat steps 1 and 2 for Cat 1, using the fabric pieces for Cat 3 and background N and Q. Sew background unit B/Q to the left side of Cat 3.

2. Using the tail pattern for Cat 3 on page 90 and 6 each of light print V and cat-fabric C, piece the tail as directed for Cat 1 in steps 3–8. Note that the direction of the strips is reversed for this cat.

After trimming, the piece should measure 1½" x 14½". Sew the tail to the left edge of the completed cat body unit.

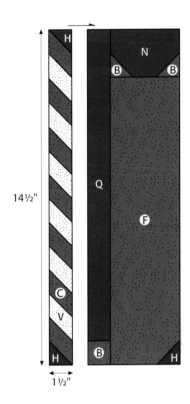

3. Add background R to the top and bottom edges and press as directed.

4. Piece the remainder of the tail as described in steps 10–12 for Cat 1, *but make it a mirror image of the tail for Cat 1.* Add background J to the top edge and press as directed.

5. Sew the tail for Cat 1 to the left edge of background S. Add the tail for Cat 3 to the right edge. Press the seams toward the background piece.

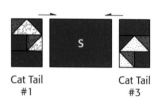

Cat Tail #1   Cat Tail #3

6. Sew the tail unit from step 5 to the top edge of Cat 2. Press toward the cat.

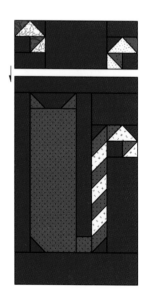

Assembling the Quilt Top

1. Referring to the illustration below, sew the completed cat units together.

2. Sew the top and bottom border strips T to the quilt top, followed by side border strips U. Press all seams toward the border strips.

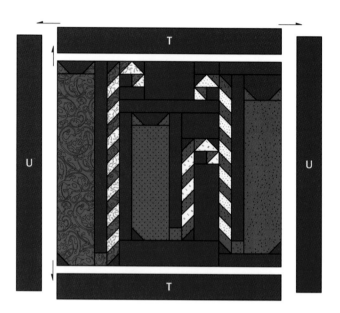

Finishing

Refer to "Finishing the Quilt" on pages 14–16.

1. Referring to "Adding Details" on page 16 and using the patterns on page 90, embroider the cat faces. Use 3 strands of embroidery floss and the stem stitch for the mouths. Make French knots for the eyes.

2. Layer the quilt top with batting and backing, and then baste the layers together.

3. Quilt around each cat.

4. Bind the quilt and add a label.

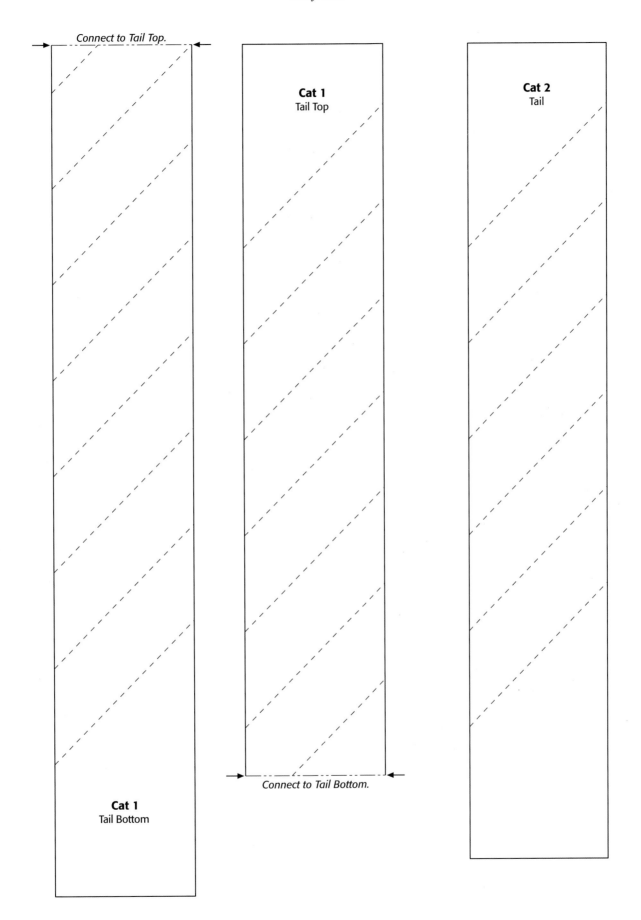

Connect to Tail Top.

Cat 1
Tail Top

Cat 2
Tail

Connect to Tail Bottom.

Cat 1
Tail Bottom

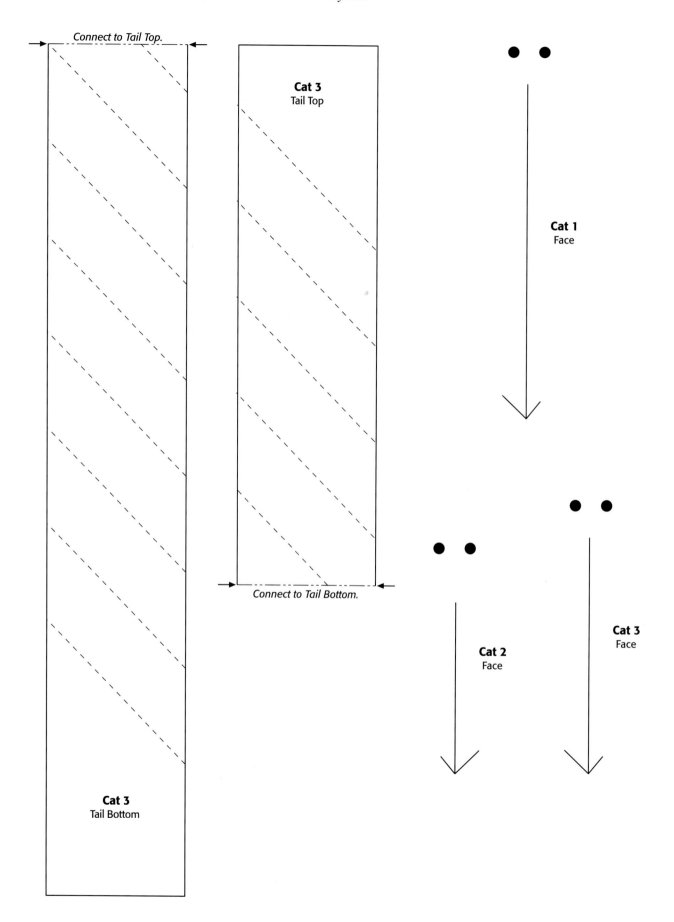

Snowdogs

*Like snowmen only different, these winter dogs sport
jaunty mufflers and warm boots and mittens.*

22" x 28", by Janet Kime

Finished Quilt: 22" x 28"
Finished Block: 6" x 8"

Snowdog Block

Materials

Yardage is based on 42"-wide fabric, with 40" of usable width after preshrinking.

Assorted fabric scraps for snowdogs, mufflers, mittens, and boots

⅔ yd. *total* assorted plaids for background blocks; fabric pieces should be at least 8" x 10" each

1 yd. plaid for border and binding

¾ yd. for backing

23" x 29" piece of batting

Black embroidery floss

Optional: Ultra Suede scraps for appliqués

Cutting

See "Making the Blocks" at right for appliqué cutting directions.

Background

Piece	No. of Pieces	Dimensions
Appliqué blocks	9	7" x 9"

Border and Binding

Cut all strips parallel to the selvages.

Piece	No. of Pieces	Dimensions
Side borders	2	2½" x 24½"
Top and bottom borders	2	2½" x 22½"
Binding	3	2¾" x 40"

Making the Blocks

Use the templates on page 95.

1. Referring to "Adding Appliqués" on pages 11–12, cut appliqué pieces A, B, C, D, E, and F for each of 9 blocks. Use the paper-patch method described on pages 11–12 to prepare the pieces for appliqué. *Do not turn under the short ends of muffler pieces D and E.* Cut and prepare 6 pairs of mittens G and 2 pairs of boots (or more if you want more snowdogs to have them). Press the prepared appliqués.

2. Referring to the photo on page 91, position the appliqués for each dog on a 7" x 9" plaid rectangle. Note that you will need to place the dog body a little to the left if the muffler ends will be on the right, and vice versa. Sew the body in place first, followed in order by the head and then the ears. There should be about ⅛" of space between the head and the body before you add muffler pieces D and E. Add muffler piece F to cover the raw edges of E. Add mittens G to 6 of the blocks, and boots H to 2 of the 6 blocks with mittens.

3. Using 2 strands of black embroidery floss, make French knots for the eyes and use a satin stitch for the nose, or cut noses from Ultra Suede scraps and appliqué with fusible web. Use 3 strands of embroidery floss and the stem stitch to embroider the stick arms and legs.

4. Press the completed blocks and trim each to 6½" x 8½".

Assembling the Quilt Top

1. Arrange the blocks in 3 horizontal rows of 3 blocks each. Sew together in rows and press the seams in opposite directions from row to row.
2. Sew the rows together and press the seams in one direction.
3. Referring to "Adding Borders" on page 13, sew the side borders to the quilt top, followed by the top and bottom borders. Press all seams toward the borders.

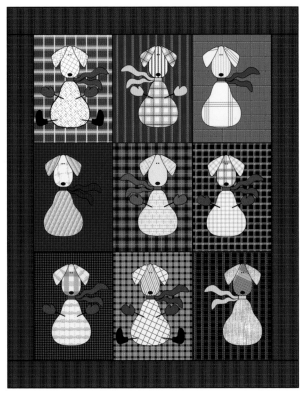

Quilt Plan

Dog Talk

Staggered Appliqué

In a whimsical quilt like this one, consider varying the design placement from block to block. In the sample quilt, the dogs weren't centered on the background pieces; some were moved to the right and some to the left. For even more interest, you could also place the dogs a little higher or lower on some of the background blocks. In the spaces created by placing the dogs off-center, you can add fancy quilting designs or embellishments, such as big sequin snowflakes, buttons shaped like dog bones, or real dog-license "charms."

Finishing

Refer to "Finishing the Quilt" on pages 14–16.

1. Layer the quilt top with batting and backing, and then baste the layers together.
2. Hand or machine quilt around each dog and in-the-ditch between the blocks and between the blocks and border.
3. Bind the quilt and add a label.

Snowdog Ornament

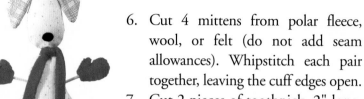

Use fabric scraps and the appliqué patterns on page 95 to make a snowdog ornament. You'll need a handful of polyester fiberfill for stuffing; round toothpicks for the "arms"; polar fleece, felt, or tightly woven wool scraps for the mittens and muffler; and clear nylon thread for hanging.

1. With fabric pieces right sides together, trace around the body, head, and ear templates. Cut out the pieces, adding seam allowances all around.

2. Stitch the pieces together on the drawn lines, leaving 1"-long openings for turning. Trim the seam allowances to ⅛" and clip the inside curves. Turn the pieces right side out, and then slipstitch the ear openings closed. Stuff the body and head lightly with fiberfill, and then slipstitch the openings closed.

3. Tack the ears to the head. Embroider the dog's eyes and nose.

4. Make a ⅛"-long slit in the center of the head at the bottom edge, and another at the top of the body. Use a toothpick to poke a hole through each slit and enlarge the holes, pushing down into the fiberfill. Remove the toothpick. Push a large drop of white glue into both holes.

5. Cut a ¾" length of toothpick. Push an end of the toothpick securely into the head, and insert the other end securely in the body, leaving about ⅛" of toothpick showing between the head and the body. Set aside to dry.

6. Cut 4 mittens from polar fleece, wool, or felt (do not add seam allowances). Whipstitch each pair together, leaving the cuff edges open.

7. Cut 2 pieces of toothpick, 2" long. Dip one end of each toothpick in white glue and push the end into a mitten. Make a ⅛" slit in each side of the dog's body. Use the end of a toothpick to poke through each slit and enlarge the holes, pushing down into the fiberfill. Push a large drop of white glue into each hole and push the other end of each mitten toothpick into the dog's body.

8. Cut a ⅜" x 6" strip for the muffler. Knot it around the toothpick neck.

9. Hang the ornament from a loop of clear nylon thread.

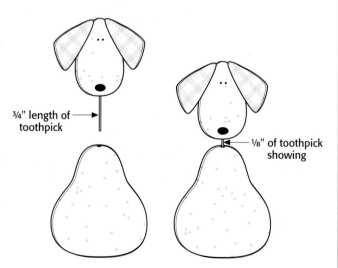

¾" length of toothpick

⅛" of toothpick showing

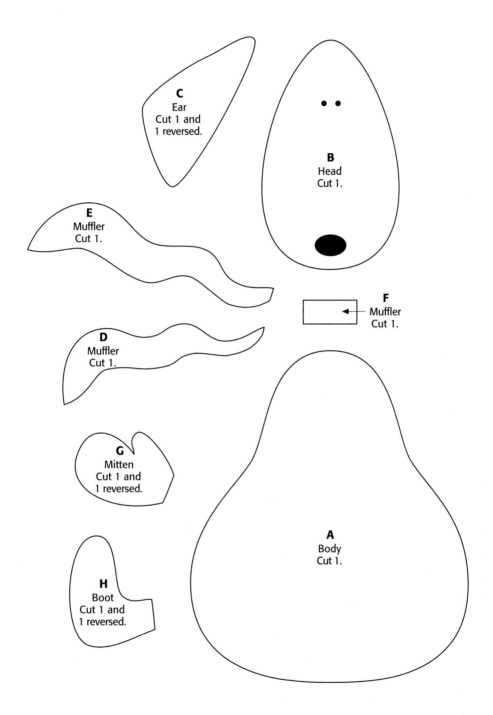

C
Ear
Cut 1 and
1 reversed.

B
Head
Cut 1.

E
Muffler
Cut 1.

F
Muffler
Cut 1.

D
Muffler
Cut 1.

G
Mitten
Cut 1 and
1 reversed.

A
Body
Cut 1.

H
Boot
Cut 1 and
1 reversed.

Redwork Airedales

Chains of red paw prints surround the redwork embroidery in this
Christmas wall hanging. Although the pieces in the Paw Print blocks
are small, speed piecing makes the assembly a breeze.

31" x 31", by Janet Kime

Finished Quilt: 31" x 31"
Finished Block: 7" x 7"

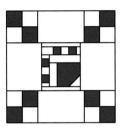

Pieced Block

Embroidered Block

Materials

Yardage is based on 42"-wide fabric, with 40" of usable width after preshrinking.

⅓ yd. *total* assorted red prints for Paw Print chain; you will need strips up to 2" wide from several different fabrics

1¼ yds. white or cream for background and borders

1 yd. for backing

⅜ yd. red print for binding

33" x 33" piece of batting

Red embroidery floss

Cutting

Paw-Print Chain

Piece	No. of Pieces	Dimensions
K	5	2" x 2"
L	4	1" x 5½"
M	7	1½" x 20"

Background, Border, and Binding

Piece	No. of Pieces	Dimensions
Redwork squares	4	8" x 8"
A	5	1¼" x 1¼"
B	5	1" x 2"
C	5	1" x 2½"
D	2	1" x 5½"
E	3	¾" x 5½"
F	1	1¼" x 5½"
G	10	¾" x 3"
H	10	2¾" x 3½"
I	14	2½" x 3½"
J	7	1½" x 20"
N	12	2½" x 2½"
O	4	2½" x 4½"
P	8	4½" x 7½"
Side borders	2	1½" x 29½"
Top and bottom borders	2	1½" x 31½"
Binding	3	2¾" x 40"

Making the Redwork Blocks

Use the embroidery templates on pages 102–103.

1. Mark the center of each 8" background square, following the directions on page 12.
2. Using a sharp pencil, lightly trace each of the redwork designs on a background square, centering the cross in each one over the center of the square.

3. Using 2 strands of red embroidery floss and the stem stitch, embroider each design.

4. Press the squares and set aside until you have completed the Paw Print blocks. The completed blocks should measure 7½" x 7½". If they don't, trim your redwork blocks to match the size of the completed Paw Print blocks. For example, if your Paw Print blocks are 7¼" x 7¼", trim the rework blocks to 7¼" x 7¼" as well. *Be sure to center the design before you trim.*

 Dog Talk

Centering the Redwork Designs

Large, square rotary rulers are great tools for trimming blocks to the required size. They're especially useful for trimming appliquéd and embroidered blocks, which often end up tilted a bit off-center. To trim the blocks for this quilt to exact 7½" squares, place strips of masking tape alongside the 7½" lines of a square rotary ruler. With a washable pen, make a cross where the 3¾" lines intersect. This corresponds to the cross in the center of the full-size embroidery designs on pages 102 and 103. Using these guides, center the design within the open area of the ruler, making sure you have a ¼"-wide seam allowance beyond the embroidery on all four sides.

Making the Paw Print Blocks and Pieced Border Units

Referring to "Flip-and-Sew Piecing" on pages 9–10 and the illustrations below, make 5 pieced Paw Print blocks.

1. Sew a background A to each red paw K. Press as directed. Make 5.

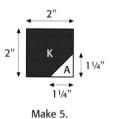

Make 5.

2. To each paw unit from step 1, add background B, followed by background C. Press as directed.

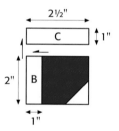

3. Using 5½"-long strips of background D and E and 2 different red strips L, assemble a strip unit as shown and press all seams toward the red strips. Crosscut 5 segments, 1" wide.

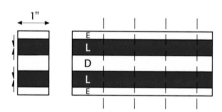

4. Sew a segment to each paw unit from step 2 and press as directed.

5. Using 5½"-long strips of background D, E, and F and 2 different red strips L, make a strip unit as shown and press as directed. Crosscut 5 segments, 1" wide.

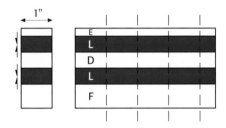

6. Sew a segment to each Paw Print unit as shown, and then add a background G to the top and bottom edges of the unit. Press as directed.

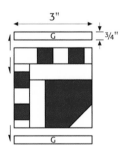

7. Sew a background H to opposite sides of each Paw Print unit.

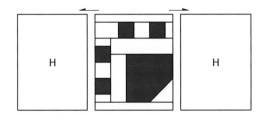

8. Using the 1½" x 20" background J and red M strips, make 7 strip units as shown. From 6 strip units, cut 12 segments, 1½" wide. Cut 4 segments from the last strip unit for a total of 76.

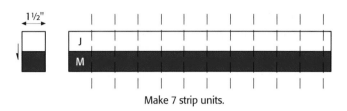

Make 7 strip units.

9. Make 36 four-patch units. Set aside the remaining two-patch segments for step 12.

Make 36
four-patch units.

10. Sew a four-patch unit to each short end of each of the 14 background I, taking care to position the colors as shown in the illustration. You should have 8 four-patch units left over for the border units.

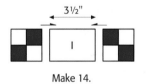

Make 14.

11. Sew a four-patch/I unit to the top and bottom edge of each of the 5 Paw Print units and press as directed. You should have 4 four-patch/background I units left for step 13.

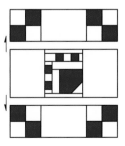

12. Sew a two-patch segment (left over from step 9) to each of 4 of the remaining four-patch units and press. Add a background N to opposite edges of the resulting six-patch units.

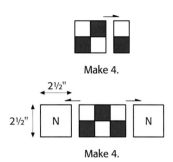

Make 4.

Make 4.

13. Sew each of the resulting six-patch units to one of the remaining four-patch/background I units and press as directed. Pay careful attention to color placement so that the red squares touch point to point.

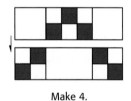

Make 4.

14. Sew a background N to each of the 4 remaining four-patch units and add a background O to the top edge of each resulting unit. Press all seams toward the background pieces.

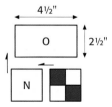

 Dog Talk ──────────

Grading Seams

When one of the fabrics in your quilt is white, darker fabrics can show through when the seam allowances are pressed toward the white fabric (as is required in this quilt). To minimize seam show-through, grade the seam of the darker fabric by trimming away a sliver of the dark seam allowance as shown.

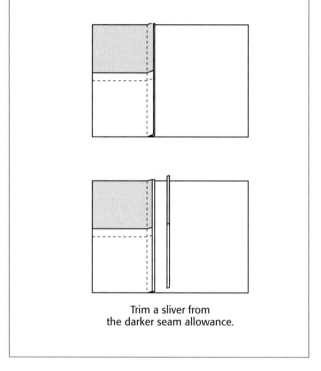

Trim a sliver from
the darker seam allowance.

Assembling the Quilt Top

1. Arrange the blocks in 3 rows of 3 blocks each, adding background P and pieced border units to the outer edges of the rows as shown on the facing page. Sew together in rows and press the seams toward the redwork squares and the background pieces. Press as directed.

2. Sew the rows together and press the seams in one direction.

3. Referring to "Adding Borders" on page 13, add the side borders, followed by the top and bottom borders. Press all seams toward the borders.

Finishing

Refer to "Finishing the Quilt" on pages 14–16.

1. Layer the quilt top with batting and backing, and then baste the layers together.

2. Hand or machine quilt in diagonal lines through the red chains and Paw Print blocks. Quilt around each redwork design and quilt paw prints in the border, using the quilting template on page 103.

3. Bind the quilt and add a label.

Redwork Airedale Ornament

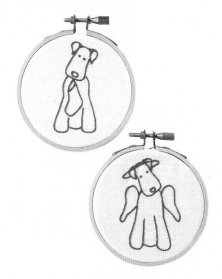

Embroider the smaller Airedales (page 102) on muslin and enclose in 3" wooden embroidery hoops to make ornaments for your tree.

1. Place the *inner ring* of a 3" wooden embroidery hoop on another piece of muslin and draw a circle, using the inside of the ring as a guide.

2. Cut out the circle, adding a ¼"-wide turn-under allowance all around. Turn under and baste the allowance; press.

3. Center the embroidered design in the hoop with the screw closure at the top and tighten the outer hoop.

4. Trim away the excess fabric on the back, leaving a generous ¼" all around.

5. Pin the muslin circle in place on the back of the hoop, covering the raw edges. Slipstitch in place. (See illustrations on page 72 for "Amewsing" Grace.)

6. Hang the ornament from a loop of clear nylon thread.

Use for ornament.

Use for ornament.

Use for
ornament.

Center

Center

Center

Center

Pawprint
Quilting Pattern

Center

Center

Trouble on the Door

*You'd better watch out! "Trouble" the kitten has found something new to climb.
This wall quilt combines speed piecing with traditional appliqué. Just for fun,
hang it on your front door in place of a traditional wreath.*

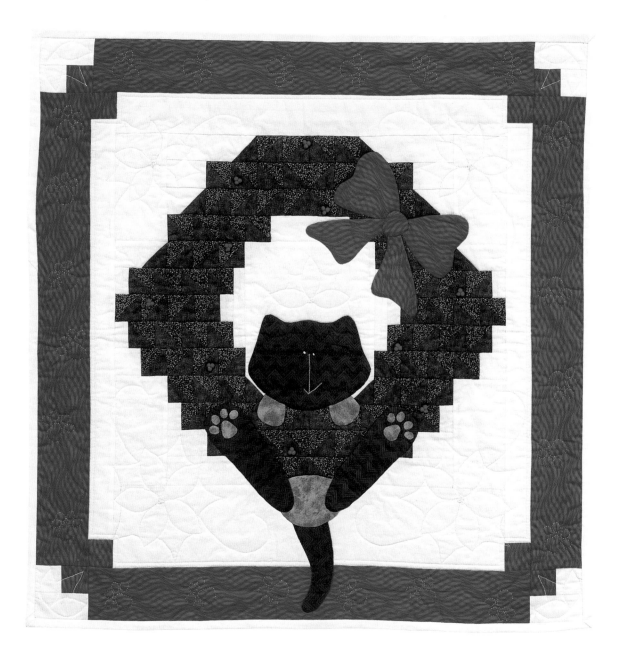

31" x 32¼", by Lorraine Herge

Materials

Yardage is based on 42"-wide fabric, with 40" of usable width after preshrinking.

⅓ yd. medium green tone-on-tone print for wreath

⅓ yd. dark green tone-on-tone print for wreath

1¼ yds. light tone-on-tone print for background and binding

¼ yd. black tone-on-tone print for cat

¼ yd. light brown tone-on-tone print for hind feet

¼ yd. red tone-on-tone print for bow

½ yd. red for border

1 yd. for backing

32" x 34" piece of batting

White embroidery floss

30 red pompons, ⅛" diameter, for berries

Cutting

Medium Green for Wreath

	No. of Pieces	Dimensions
	47	2⅜" x 2⅜"

Dark Green for Wreath

	No. of Pieces	Dimensions
	47	2⅜" x 2⅜"
	8	2" x 2"

Background

Piece	No. of Pieces	Dimensions
A	1	8" x 8"
B	1	2" x 8"
C	1	2" x 5"
D	2	1¼" x 5"
E	8	1¼" x 2"
F	6	2" x 2"
G	6	2" x 2¾"
H	6	2" x 3½"
I	4	2" x 5¾"
J	4	3½" x 6½"
K	1	2¾" x 23"
L	1	5" x 23"
M	2	2" x 23¾"

Border and Binding

Piece	No. of Pieces	Dimensions
N	8	2" x 2"
O	2	3½" x 26"
P	2	3½" x 26¾"
Binding	4	2¾" x 40"

Making the Quilt Top

Referring to "Making Half-Square-Triangle Units" on page 10 and the illustrations below, piece the required units for the quilt top.

1. Using the medium and dark green 2⅜" squares, make 94 half-square-triangle units.

Sew 47 pairs.

2. Sew 4 half-square triangles together as shown to make 9 identical strip units and 9 mirror-image units. Press as directed.

Make 9.   Make 9.

3. Sew a 2" dark green square to the end of background I. Make 1 and 1 reversed. Add 2 half-square-triangle units to each unit, positioning the seams as shown.

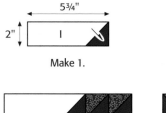

Make 1.   Make 1.

Make 1.   Make 1.

4. Sew a 2" dark green square to the end of background G. Make 1 and 1 reversed.

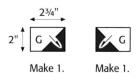

Make 1.   Make 1.

5. Arrange and sew the units from steps 2–4, background C, and background G together in horizontal rows as shown. Press as directed.

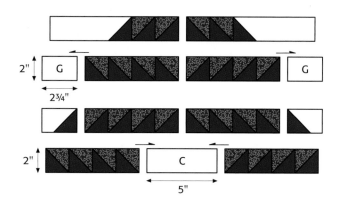

6. Add background J to opposite sides of the resulting unit, followed by background K. Press as directed. Set wreath top section aside.

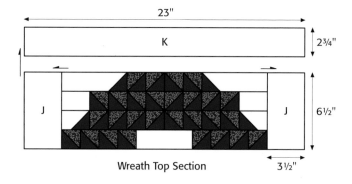

Wreath Top Section

7. Sew a dark green square to the end of background H. Make 1 and 1 reversed.

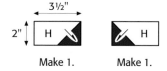

Make 1.   Make 1.

8. Using 3 strip units from step 2, plus 3 background E and 1 background D, arrange the pieces for the left side of the wreath and sew

together as shown. Press as directed. Make a mirror image for the right side of the wreath.

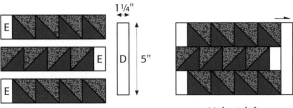

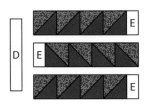 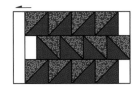

Make 1 left
wreath side section.

Make 1 right
wreath side section.

9. Arrange the units from steps 7 and 8 with additional half-square-triangle units, 1 of the triangle strip units from step 2, and background F to complete each wreath side section. Press as directed.

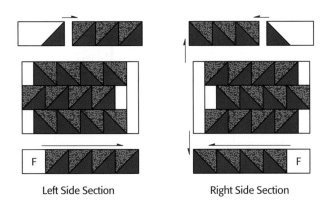

Left Side Section   Right Side Section

10. Sew the resulting units to opposite sides of background A and press. Set the completed center section aside.

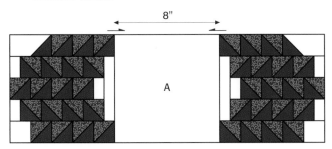

Wreath Center Section

11. Sew a dark green 2" square to opposite ends of background B.

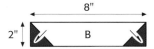

12. Using the remaining half-square-triangle units from step 1, the remaining triangle strip units from step 2, and the remaining background E, G, and I, arrange and sew together the pieces for each row of the bottom section of the wreath. Press as directed. Sew the rows together and press.

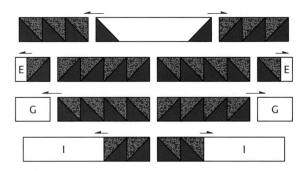

13. Add a background J to each short end; add background L to the lower edge. Press as directed.

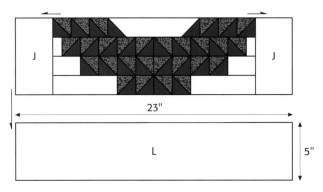

Wreath Bottom Section

14. Sew the wreath sections together and press as directed.

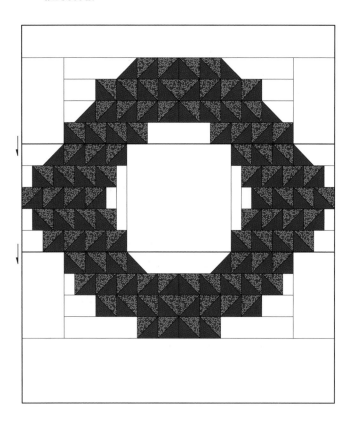

Adding the Borders

1. Sew a border square N to the ends of each background M. Press.

Make 2.

Sew the resulting border strips to opposite sides of the wreath. Add the top and bottom borders O. Press all seams toward the border strips.

2. Using border pieces N and the remaining F and H background pieces, make 2 corner units and 2 reversed. Press as directed.

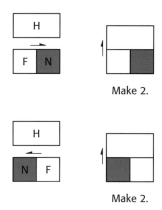

3. Sew a corner unit to each end of each border piece P, taking care to position so the red square is at the inner corner of each strip. Sew the completed outer side borders to the quilt top.

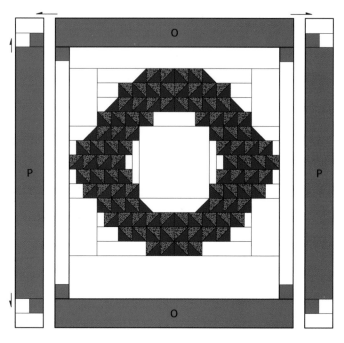

Adding the Appliqués

Use the templates on pages 110–111.

1. Referring to "Adding Appliqués" on pages 11–12, prepare the bow and kitten appliqué pieces. Leave the straight edge of each of the 4 bow pieces AA and BB and the straight edges of each front paw DD and tail FF unturned.

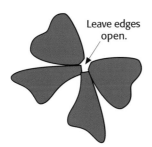

Leave edges open.

2. Position the bow on the quilt top in the upper right corner of the wreath and sew in place, adding the knot piece CC last to cover the raw edges of the bow pieces.

3. Position and appliqué the cat front paws, then the head, covering the raw edges of the paws.

4. Position and appliqué the cat tail FF, then the tummy GG, covering the raw edge of the tail.

5. Position and appliqué the foot and toe pads II and JJ to each hind foot HH. Position and sew each hind foot in place.

6. Embroider the cat face with 3 strands of embroidery floss, making French knots for eyes and using the stem stitch for the nose and mouth.

Finishing

Refer to "Finishing the Quilt" on pages 14–16.

1. Layer the quilt top with batting and backing, and then baste the layers together.

2. Quilt as desired. In the sample quilt, large poinsettias were quilted in each outer corner beyond the wreath, and paw prints were quilted in the borders. See page 103 for a paw-print quilting template.

3. Group the red pompons in 10 sets of 3 each and sew to the wreath.

4. Bind the quilt and add a label.

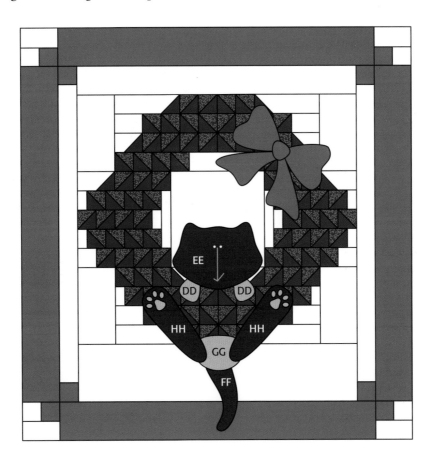

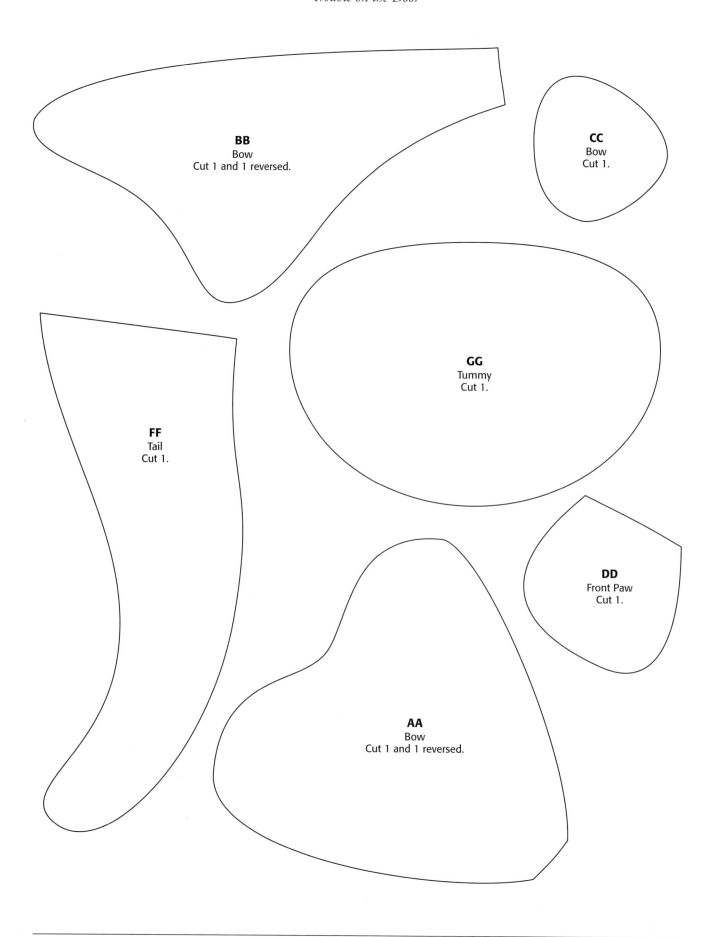

BB
Bow
Cut 1 and 1 reversed.

CC
Bow
Cut 1.

GG
Tummy
Cut 1.

FF
Tail
Cut 1.

DD
Front Paw
Cut 1.

AA
Bow
Cut 1 and 1 reversed.

EE
Face
Cut 1.

←———— Straight of grain ————→

HH
Hind Foot
Cut 2.

←——————————→

JJ
Toe Pad
Cut 8.

II
Foot Pad
Cut 2.

About the Author

Janet Kime is a talented quiltmaker and designer who has written five other books for Martingale & Company, including the bestselling *The Cat's Meow*. She and her goats live on rural Vashon Island in Washington State, where several cats allow her to share their home.